Collins

SNAP

REVISION

WORKBOOK

UNSEEN POETRY

GCSE 9-1 English Literature

For AQA

RENÉE STANTON

BE EXAM-READY IN A SNAP

Published by Collins
An imprint of HarperCollins*Publishers*
1 London Bridge Street
London SE1 9GF

© HarperCollins*Publishers* Limited 2019

ISBN 9780008355319

First published 2019

10 9 8 7 6 5 4 3 2

Commissioning Editor: Claire Souza
Managing Editor: Shelley Teasdale
Author: Renée Stanton
Copyeditor and project management: Fiona Watson
Typesetting: Jouve India Private Limited
Cover designers: Kneath Associates and Sarah Duxbury
Inside concept design: Ian Wrigley
Illustrations: Rose and Thorn Creative Services Ltd
Production: Karen Nulty
Printed in the UK by Martins the Printer Ltd.

ACKNOWLEDGEMENTS

p.17, 'The Farrier' from *Skirrid Hill* by Owen Sheers. Published by Seren Books, 2005. Copyright © Owen Sheers. Reproduced by permission of Owen Sheers c/o Rogers, Coleridge & White Ltd., 20 Powis Mews, London W11 1JN; p.25, 'To My Nine-Year-Old-Self' by Helen Dunmore from *Counting Backwards: Poems 1975-2017* (Bloodaxe Books, 2019); p.30, 'Genetics' from *The State of the Prisons* by Sinead Morrissey. Published by Carcanet Press Ltd, 2005; p.37, 'Very Simply Topping Up the Brake Fluid' by Simon Armitage from *Zoom!* (Bloodaxe Books, 1989); p.40, 'Being Boring' by Wendy Cope, reproduced by permission of Faber & Faber Ltd; p.46, 'Tamer and Hawk' by Thom Gunn, reproduced by permission of Faber & Faber Ltd; p.52, 'Twice Shy' by Seamus Heaney, reproduced by permission of Faber & Faber Ltd.

The author and publisher are grateful to the copyright holders for permission to use quoted materials and images.

Every effort has been made to trace copyright holders and obtain their permission for the use of copyright material. The author and publisher will gladly receive information enabling them to rectify any error or omission in subsequent editions. All facts are correct at time of going to press.

Contents

'Those Winter Sundays' by Robert Hayden

Sundays too my father got up early

and put his clothes on in the blueblack cold,

then with cracked hands that ached

from labour in the weekday weather made

banked fires blaze. No one ever thanked him.

I'd wake and hear the cold splintering, breaking.

When the rooms were warm, he'd call,

and slowly I would rise and dress,

fearing the chronic angers of that house,

Speaking indifferently to him,

who had driven out the cold

and polished my good shoes as well.

What did I know, what did I know

of love's austere[1] and lonely offices[2]?

[1]severe, strict or stern; [2]help given to or services done for others

Revise 1

Develop some questions to ask about the poem. Here is one to get you started: Who is the speaker?

_____

_____

_____

Revise 2

Find five quotations that relate to the father's actions and five quotations that relate to the speaker's actions/thoughts/feelings. Record the examples below in two lists. Does this help you to identify a theme?

What do the following lines or sentences tell you about the themes of the poem?

a) 'Sundays too my father got up early ...'

_____

_____

b) 'No one ever thanked him.'

_____

_____

c) 'fearing the chronic angers of that house ...'

_____

_____

d) 'Speaking indifferently to him ...'

_____

_____

e) 'and polished my good shoes as well.'

_____

_____

Extend

Look at the whole poem and write one paragraph on the way the father is represented, and one paragraph on the way the speaker represents himself.

Active Learning

Imagine you were asked to interview the poet, Robert Hayden. What questions would you ask him about this poem?

Write about the meaning of the following images and what they have in common.

  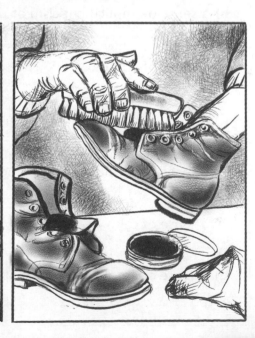

'Composed on Westminster Bridge, September 3, 1802' by William Wordsworth

Earth has not anything to show more fair:

Dull would he be of soul who could pass by

A sight so touching in its majesty;

This city now doth, like a garment, wear

The beauty of the morning; silent, bare,

Ships, towers, domes, theatres and temples lie

Open unto the fields and to the sky;

All bright and glittering in the smokeless air.

Never did sun more beautifully steep

In his first splendour, valley, rock or hill;

Ne'er saw I, never felt a calm so deep!

The river glideth at his own sweet will:

Dear God! The very houses seem asleep

And all that mighty heart is lying still!

Revise 1

Select quotations that communicate mood and tone by conveying:

a) a sense of awe/admiration

_____

b) a sense of implicit criticism of the reader

_____

c) a sense of wonder

_____

d) a sense of beauty

_____

e) a sense of confiding something

_____

f) a sense of calm

_____

g) a sense of emphasis/exaggeration

_____

Revise 2

Explain how the following lines express a sense of quiet or slowness, or both.

a)

> ... silent, bare,
> Ships, towers, domes, theatres and temples lie
> Open unto the fields and to the sky ...

....

....

....

b)

> The river glideth at his own sweet will ...

....

....

....

c)

> Dear God! The very houses seem asleep
> And all that mighty heart is lying still!

....

....

....

Revise 3

Think about the mood and tone of the poem. Write one paragraph on the first eight lines, and one paragraph on the last six lines. Make sure you comment on the extent to which the tone and mood stays stable or shifts.

....

....

....

....

....

....

....

....

....

....

....

....

....

....

....

....

....

....

Extend

Write a sentence explaining how each of the following affect the mood and tone of the poem:

a) the perspective of the speaker

b) the setting

c) the imagery

d) the language.

Active Learning

Look closely at this photograph of Westminster Bridge taken in the early morning, reflecting today's London. What would Wordsworth think of the view? Write down your thoughts with reference to the poem.

Which lines of the poem could be represented in the following images?

'The Pike' by Amy Lowell

In the brown water,

Thick and silver-sheened in the sunshine,

Liquid and cool in the shade of the reeds,

A pike dozed.

Lost among the shadows of stems

He lay unnoticed.

Suddenly he flicked his tail,

And a green-and-copper brightness

Ran under the water.

Out from under the reeds

Came the olive-green light,

And orange flashed up

Through the sun-thickened water.

So the fish passed across the pool,

Green and copper,

A darkness and a gleam,

And the blurred reflections of the willows on the opposite bank

Received it.

Revise 1

Identify words relating to the following semantic fields. List them in the order they appear in the poem:

a) colour

....

....

b) light/darkness

....

....

c) movement/stillness (the verbs will help you here)

....

....

d) natural world.

....

....

Think about the two sections of the poem with regard to the semantic fields of movement/stillness, light/darkness and colour.

a) How does the pike's movement change as the poem develops?

....

....

....

....

....

b) Are there any words which give the pike human qualities?

....

....

....

....

....

c) How do the light/dark words change as the poem develops?

....

....

....

....

....

d) How does the poet use language to depict colour with accuracy?

....

....

....

....

....

a) The sound quality of some of the words in this poem complements the visual images and helps to establish a mood. Make a note of the:

(i) whispering sibilant /s/ and /sh/ sounds

....

....

....

....

(ii) long vowel sounds, which suggest a pleasurable sense of inactivity.

....

....

....

....

b) Write a paragraph on how the patterns of sound enhance the visual qualities of the poem.

....

....

....

....

Extend

Some of the words provide more than a precise and colourful image of a pike, its territory and the way it moves. They inject a sense of mystery and drama. Identify these words and write a paragraph about their effect.

Active Learning

Create a learning poster by collecting different images of pikes. Annotate your poster with lines from the poem.

Which lines of the poem could be represented in the following images?

'Solitude' by Babette Deutsch

There is the loneliness of peopled places:

Streets roaring with their human flood; the crowd

That fills bright rooms with billowing sounds and faces,

Like foreign music, overshrill and loud.

There is the loneliness of one who stands

Fronting the waste[1] under the cold sea-light,

A wisp of flesh against the endless sands,

Like a lost gull in solitary flight.

Single is all up-rising and down-lying;

Struggle or fear or silence none may share;

Each is alone in bearing and in dying;

Conquest is uncompanioned as despair.

Yet I have known no loneliness like this,

Locked in your arms and bent beneath your kiss.

[1]somewhere vast and uninhabited

Revise 1

This poem is a Shakespearian sonnet. Explore how the fourteen lines are organised.

a) Use a letter notation to indicate the pattern of the rhyme scheme.

....

b) How many quatrains are there?

....

c) Where is the rhyming couplet?

....

a) Indicate whether each of the following lines **introduces**, **develops** or **changes the direction** of the theme of solitude.

  (i) 'Yet I have known no loneliness like this ...' ....

 (ii) 'There is the loneliness of peopled places ...' ....

(iii) 'There is the loneliness of one who stands ...' ....

(iv) 'Single is all up-rising and down-lying ...' ....

b) Which words/phrases convey that loneliness can be experienced:

(i) with others?

....

....

(ii) away from others?

....

....

Write three paragraphs, one on each quatrain, exploring the key ideas and imagery. Identify the links between the first and second quatrain and between the second and third quatrain.

....

....

....

....

....

....

....

....

....

....

....

....

....

....

....

_____

_____

_____

_____

_____

_____

Extend

The rhyming couplet changes the poem. Write a paragraph exploring how:

- the earlier ideas of the poem are cancelled out

- the speaker is experiencing a whole new kind of loneliness or is no longer lonely

- the imagery changes.

Active Learning

Create a collage to reflect some of the images of loneliness conveyed in the sonnet. Anchor the images with lines from the poem.

Describe the different mood and atmosphere shown in each of the following images.

'Funeral Blues' by W.H. Auden

Stop all the clocks, cut off the telephone,

Prevent the dog from barking with a juicy bone,

Silence the pianos and with muffled drum

Bring out the coffin, let the mourners come.

Let aeroplanes circle overhead

Scribbling on the sky the message He Is Dead,

Put crêpe bows round the white necks of public doves,

Let the traffic policemen wear black cotton gloves.

He was my North, my South, my East and West,

My working week and my Sunday rest,

My noon, my midnight, my talk, my song;

I thought that love would last for ever: I was wrong.

The stars are not wanted now: put out every one;

Pack up the moon and dismantle the sun;

Pour away the ocean and sweep up the wood.

For nothing now can ever come to any good.

> ### Revise 1

This poem tells a story of a funeral and what the bereaved speaker is thinking and feeling. Identify quotations which describe the speaker's:

a) love for the deceased

....

b) feeling of grief/loss/lack of purpose

....

c) ideas for eliminating distractions from the funeral

....

d) feelings that the world should share the grief

....

e) surreal thoughts about what the universe should do to mourn

....

The poem makes use of several lists in the telling of the story.

a) Use different colours to highlight the lists of:

   (i) commands (look at the verbs)

   (ii) requests (look at the verbs)

   (iii) descriptions of what the deceased man means to the speaker.

b) What do the lists add to the story?

....

....

....

....

Revise 3

Each quatrain plays a role in the story telling. Write four brief paragraphs explaining how each quatrain adds to the story.

....

....

....

....

....

....

....

....

....

....

....

Extend

How does mood and tone shift as the story unfolds? Write a paragraph.

Active Learning

View the clip of John Hannah reading this poem in the film *Four Weddings and a Funeral*. Think about how the experience of seeing and hearing him perform the poem adds to your understanding.

'The Farrier' by Owen Sheers

Blessing himself with his apron,

the leather black and tan of a rain-beaten bay[1],

he pitches a roll-up to his lips and waits

for the mare to be led from the field to the yard,

the smoke slow-turning from his mouth

and the wind twisting his sideburns in its fingers.

She smells him as he passes, woodbine[2], metal and hoof,

careful not to look her in the eye as he runs his hand

the length of her neck, checking for dust on a lintel.

Folding her back leg with one arm, he leans into her flank

like a man putting his shoulder to a knackered car,

catches the hoof between his knees

as if it's always just fallen from a table,

cups her fetlock and bends,

a romantic lead dropping to the lips of his lover.

Then the close work begins: cutting moon-silver clippings,

excavating the arrow head of her frog[3],

filing at her sole and branding on a shoe

in an apparition of smoke,

three nails gritted between his teeth,

a seamstress pinning the dress of the bride.

Placing his tools in their beds,

he gives her a slap and watches her leave,

awkward in her new shoes, walking on strange ground.

The sound of his steel, biting at her heels.

[1] a brown horse with a black mane, tail and lower legs; [2] a type of cigarette, now discontinued; [3] part of a horse's hoof, triangular in shape

This poem, written in the third person, is an extended description of a farrier at work. The poet uses the third-person perspective in an objective way, like a camera recording what can be seen. The reader does not know what the farrier is thinking and feeling and can only make judgements about him through his appearance, actions and behaviour.

Use different colours to highlight language which:

a) describes the farrier's appearance

b) describes the farrier's actions, skills, confidence and experience

c) suggests he is a mysterious figure

d) suggests his attitude to the mare.

Consider the following language, associated with the mare.

she smells him	awkward in her new shoes, walking on strange ground		
her neck	her back leg	her flank	her fetlock
her frog	her sole	his lover	the bride
	led from the field to the yard		

Write a paragraph exploring how the poet keeps the image of the mare's femaleness in the reader's mind and who the mare is compared to. What poetic devices are used to do this?

Write a paragraph explaining how the following descriptions associate the farrier with the natural world.

> **his apron, / the leather black and tan of a rain-beaten bay**
>
> **the wind twisting his sideburns**
>
> **The sound of his steel, biting at her heels.**

Extend

Write a paragraph about the way in which the farrier is presented in the poem.

Active Learning

Find some images of farriers at work. Explore what the reality of a forge with all its tools and equipment looks like. To what extent is the poem realistic?

Which lines of the poem could be represented in the following images?

'Holy Thursday' by William Blake

'Twas on a Holy Thursday[1], their innocent faces clean,

The children walking two and two, in red and blue and green[2],

Grey-headed beadles[3] walk'd before, with wands as white as snow

Till into the high dome of Paul's[4], they like Thames' waters flow.

O what a multitude they seem'd, these flowers of London Town!

Seated in companies they sit with radiance all their own.

The hum of multitudes was there, but multitudes of lambs,

Thousands of little boys and girls raising their innocent hands.

Now like a mighty wind, they raise to heaven the voice of song

Or like harmonious thunderings the seats of heaven among.

Beneath them sit the aged men, wise guardians of the poor;

Then cherish pity, lest you drive an angel from your door.

[1] Ascension Day, which commemorates Jesus Christ's ascension into heaven, according to Christian belief;
[2] 'in red and blue and green' refers to the colours of the children's school coats; [3] officials who take part in the ceremony;
[4] a cathedral in London

> **Revise 1**

This poem is a ballad of three quatrains telling the story of an annual service in St Paul's Cathedral. The six thousand children attended London charity schools. They stood on specially erected scaffolds.

Write a paragraph exploring how the following words and phrases from the poem create an image of the children's purity and beauty.

innocent faces clean	like Thames' waters flow	these flowers of London Town!
with radiance all their own	multitudes of lambs	raising their innocent hands
	like a mighty wind like harmonious thunderings	

There are several patterns of sound in the ballad which contribute to its lively rhythm. What do you notice about the following?

a) the rhyme scheme

_____

b) the number of syllables per line

_____

c) the pattern of stressed and unstressed syllables

_____

Revise 3

Write a paragraph about how the story of the event is described, looking closely at the focus of each quatrain.

_____

_____

_____

_____

_____

_____

_____

Extend

Look closely at the final line. How is it different from the other lines? Who is the 'you' being addressed and what is being communicated? Write a short paragraph on the effect of the final line.

Active Learning

Find out more about charity schools in the 18th century and create a learning poster to record your findings.

Which lines of the poem could be represented in the following images?

'Manwatching' by Georgia Garrett

From across the party I watch you,

Watching her.

Do my possessive eyes

Imagine your silent messages?

I think not.

She looks across at you

And telegraphs her flirtatious reply.

I have come to recognise this code,

You are on intimate terms with this pretty stranger,

And there is nothing I can do,

My face is calm, expressionless,

But my eyes burn into your back

While my insides shout with rage.

She weaves her way towards you,

Turning on a bewitching smile.

I can't see your face, but you are mesmerised, I expect.

I can predict you: I know this scene so well,

Some acquaintance grabs your arm,

You turn and meet my accusing stare head on.

Her eyes follow yours, meet mine,

And then slide away, she understands,

She's not interested enough to compete.

It's over now.

She fades away, you drift towards me,

'I'm bored' you say, without a trace of guilt,

So we go.

Passing the girl in the hall,

'Bye' I say frostily.

I suppose

You winked.

This poem, written from the first-person perspective, describes the observations, thoughts and feelings of a young woman at a party. The reader has a direct and intimate knowledge of the speaker's mind at work but only sees and understands what the female speaker sees and understands.

Underline five lines which communicate the perspective of the poem. (The semantic field of looking/watching/eyes will help you here.)

Revise 2

a) What do the following quotations communicate about the speaker's thoughts, feelings and judgements?

(i) '... my possessive eyes ...'

(ii) 'I think not.'

(iii) 'Turning on a bewitching smile.'

(iv) '... but you are mesmerised, I expect.'

(v) 'She's not interested enough to compete.'

(vi) '... without a trace of guilt ...'

b) What do the following quotations communicate about the nature of this situation?

- 'I have come to recognise this code ...'
- 'I can predict you: I know this scene so well ...'

There are two short pieces of dialogue in the poem. What does the dialogue convey and how does it reinforce or challenge your impression of the speaker?

_____

_____

_____

_____

Extend

Write a paragraph on the effects of the first-person perspective.

Active Learning

Explore the idea of non-verbal communication. What kinds of emotions, thoughts and feelings can be communicated by the eyes and the face? Make a poster of your findings and find supporting illustrations/images.

Create a fourth panel for this comic strip showing what happens next, either between the two main characters or with the others back at the party.

'To My Nine-Year-Old-Self' by Helen Dunmore

You must forgive me. Don't look so surprised,

perplexed, and eager to be gone,

balancing on your hands or on the tightrope.

You would rather run than walk, rather climb than run

rather leap from a height than anything.

I have spoiled this body we once shared.

Look at the scars, and watch the way I move,

careful of a bad back or a bruised foot.

Do you remember how, three minutes after waking,

we'd jump straight out of the ground floor window

into the summer morning?

That dream we had, no doubt it's as fresh in your mind

as the white paper to write it on.

We made a start, but something else came up –

a baby vole, or a bag of sherbet lemons –

and besides, that summer of ambition

created an icy lolly factory, a wasp trap

and a den by the cesspit.

I'd like to say we could be friends

but the truth is we have nothing in common

beyond a few shared years. I won't keep you then.

Time to pick rosehips for tuppence a pound,

time to hide down scared lanes

from men in cars after girl-children,

Or to lunge out over the water

on a rope that swings from that tree

long buried in housing –

but no, I shan't cloud your morning. God knows

I have fears enough for us both –

I leave you in an ecstasy of concentration

slowly peeling a ripe scab from your knee

to taste it on your tongue.

In this poem, the perspective is that of a female speaker ('I') addressing her younger self ('you') as if in conversation. Sometimes the speaker refers to them both as 'we'. The pronouns are important in establishing the perspective.

Use different colours to underline some examples of where:

a) the speaker's nine-year-old-self is separate from her older self

b) the speaker's nine-year-old-self is temporarily unified with her older self.

What semantic fields are associated with the self who is:

a) the nine-year-old girl?

b) the older woman?

The second-person address means that the poem sounds conversational, although we only hear the one voice. There are several shifts in tone and conversational patterns.

a) Find quotations where the speaker sounds:

(i) nostalgic

(ii) apologetic

(iii) gently reprimanding

(iv) realistic.

b) Find quotations where the speaker sounds as if she is:

(i) signalling the end of the conversation

(ii) expressing something which is difficult to say.

How do you respond to the final three lines of the poem?

What would you say to your nine-year-old-self? Try writing your own one-sided poem.

Write about the images of youth depicted below and what they connote.

'What lips my lips have kissed, and where, and why' by Edna St Vincent Millay

What lips my lips have kissed, and where, and why,

I have forgotten, and what arms have lain

Under my head till morning; but the rain

Is full of ghosts tonight, that tap and sigh

Upon the glass and listen for reply,

And in my heart there stirs a quiet pain

For unremembered lads that not again

Will turn to me at midnight with a cry.

Thus in the winter stands the lonely tree,

Nor knows what birds have vanished one by one,

Yet knows its boughs more silent than before:

I cannot say what loves have come and gone,

I only know that summer sang in me

A little while, that in me sings no more.

Revise 1

Explore the first eight lines of the poem, the octave. Circle the words that best describe the speaker's state of mind/mood.

sad	forgetful	emotional	living in the past
haunted by the past		desiring love	nostalgic
romantic		yearning for her youth	

The sestet, the last six lines of the poem, explores a new line of thinking, introduced by the volta, the turning point ('Thus in the winter stands the lonely tree').

a) Explore the image of the 'lonely tree' and how it is described. How does it relate to the feelings communicated in the octave?

....

....

....

b) What do the metaphors of 'winter' and 'summer' symbolise?

....

....

....

c) Look closely at the last three lines of the sestet. How does the sonnet end?

....

....

....

....

This sonnet is mostly written in iambic pentameter, with five feet of one unstressed syllable followed by a stressed syllable. Here is an example: 'What LIPS my LIPS have KISSED and WHERE and WHY'.

a) Look closely at the volta. What do you notice about the pattern of stresses in this line?

....

....

b) What is the effect in the change of pattern?

....

....

....

Extend

Love is a conventional theme of the sonnet form. What makes this sonnet, written by Edna St Vincent Millay (1892–1950), untraditional?

Active Learning

What is it about the theme of love that makes it a favourite theme for poetry? Explore your ideas and make a learning poster.

'Genetics' by Sinead Morrissey

My father's in my fingers, but my mother's in my palms.

I lift them up and look at them with pleasure –

I know my parents made me by my hands.

They may have been repelled to separate lands,

To separate hemispheres, may sleep with other lovers,

But in me they touch, where fingers link to palms.

With nothing left of their togetherness but friends

Who quarry for their image by a river,

At least I know their marriage by my hands.

I shape a chapel where a steeple stands.

And when I turn it over,

My father's by my fingers, my mother's by my palms

demure before a priest reciting psalms.

My body is their marriage register.

I re-enact their wedding by my hands.

So take me with you, take up the skin's demands

For mirroring in bodies of the future.

I'll bequeath my fingers, if you bequeath your palms.

We know our parents make us by our hands.

Revise 1

a) This poem makes use of the device of repetition. Underline the repetitions you can see.

b) What are the main themes in the poem?

....

....

....

The repetitions help to build meaning, by making the key ideas clearer, more memorable and emphatic. The key ideas also form clusters of words with related meanings (semantic fields).

Read the following statements about the poem's key ideas or themes. Link the statements to particular lines in the poem.

a) the physical traits that children inherit from their parents

_____

b) the speaker's sadness arising from parental separation

_____

c) how a child is an ever-lasting reminder of a parental relationship

_____

d) the speaker's hope for the future, that they will have children and that their genetic inheritance will be passed on.

_____

Revise 3

Write a paragraph on how the device of repetition helps to convey the key themes of the poem.

_____

_____

_____

_____

_____

_____

_____

_____

_____

_____

Extend

How does the first-person perspective give clarity to the poem's theme? Write a paragraph.

Active Learning

The poem is made up of five tercets and a quatrain. All contain images. Make six sketches which try and reflect these images and annotate them with lines from the poem.

'Blackbird' by John Drinkwater

He comes on chosen evenings,

My blackbird bountiful[1], and sings

Over the garden of the town

Just at the hour the sun goes down.

His flight across the chimneys thick,

By some divine arithmetic,

Comes to his customary stack,

And couches[2] there his plumage black,

And there he lifts his yellow bill,

Kindled against the sunset, till

These suburbs are like Dymock[3] woods

Where music has her solitudes,

And while he mocks the winter's wrong

Rapt[4] on his pinnacle of song,

Figured above our garden plots

Those are celestial chimney-pots.

[1]generous; [2]settles/rests (literary); [3]a village in Gloucestershire; [4]completely fascinated or absorbed by what one is seeing or hearing

 Revise 1

Use different colours to underline descriptions of the blackbird's:

a) appearance

b) location.

Explore what the following quotations suggest about the blackbird:

a) 'chosen evenings' / 'blackbird bountiful' / 'customary stack'

....

....

b) 'divine arithmetic' / 'Kindled against the sunset' / 'Rapt on his pinnacle of song' / 'celestial chimney-pots'

....

....

....

Revise 3

The blackbird seems to stand for something other than himself. Write a paragraph on what you think the blackbird symbolises for the speaker.

....

....

....

....

Extend

The location of the poem is the 'suburbs', the outskirts of a town. The poet uses a simile to describe the suburbs, comparing them to 'Dymock woods / Where music has her solitudes'. Write a paragraph about the effect that the blackbird has on the speaker's sense of place.

Active Learning

Find out more about the qualities, myths and symbolism associated with the blackbird. Create a learning poster to record your findings.

Link the following images to specific lines from the poem.

'The Eagle' by Alfred Tennyson

He clasps the crag with crooked hands

Close to the sun in lonely lands

Ring'd with the azure world, he stands.

The wrinkled sea beneath him crawls

He watches from his mountain walls

And like a thunderbolt he falls.

Revise 1

a) There are several sound patterns in this short poem of two triplets: rhyme, metre, alliteration and assonance.

(i) What do you notice about the rhyme scheme? Use letters to mark out the pattern.

(ii) How many syllables are there in each line? What is the dominant stress pattern? Is it mostly 'di-dum di-dum' or 'dum-di dum-di'?

(iii) How many feet are there in the lines and what is the metre?

(iv) Are the rhyming words stressed or unstressed?

(v) Which lines start with a stressed syllable?

b) Identify whether the sound patterns shared by the following groups of words are alliteration or assonance. Discuss their effect on meaning where it feels appropriate.

(i) clasps, crag, crooked, close

(ii) crag, hands

(iii) close, lonely

....

....

(iv) lonely, lands

....

....

(v) ring'd, wrinkled

....

....

(vi) watches, walls

....

....

Revise 2

Patterns of sound help to emphasise certain words by drawing them to the reader's attention. So, as well as making the poem appealing to the reader's ear, the patterns themselves can be important to the poem's meaning.

a) Which words give the eagle a human-like quality?

....

b) Which words or phrases suggest that the eagle is high up?

....

....

c) Which words or phrases suggest the eagle's power?

....

....

Revise 3

How would you describe the poem's style? Choose some words from the box below and use them in a paragraph. Include quotations to support your answer.

plain	ornate	simple	sensuous	rich	complex	concise	precise
aural	visual	literal	metaphorical	clear	vague	unusual	

....

....

....

....

_____
_____
_____
_____

Extend

Write two paragraphs, one on each triplet, about how the eagle is described.

Active Learning

Look closely at the photograph of the eagle and re-read the final line of the poem. What do you think the poet was trying to capture about the eagle with the simile?

Which lines of the poem could be represented in the following images?

'Very Simply Topping Up the Brake Fluid' by Simon Armitage

Yes, love, that's why the warning light comes on. Don't

panic. Fetch some universal brake-fluid

and a five-eighths screwdriver from your toolkit

then prop the bonnet open. Go on, it won't

eat you. Now without slicing through the fan-belt

try and slide the sharp end of the screwdriver

under the lid and push the spade connector

through its bed, go on, that's it. Now you're all right

to unscrew, no clockwise, you see it's Russian

love, back to front, that's it. You see, it's empty.

Now gently with your hand and I mean gently,

try and create a bit of space by pushing

the float chamber sideways so there's room to pour,

gently does it, that's it. Try not to spill it, it's

corrosive: rusts, you know, and fill it till it's

level with the notch on the clutch reservoir.

Lovely. There's some Swarfega in the office

if you want a wash and some soft roll above

the cistern, for, you know. Oh don't mind him love,

he doesn't bite. Come here and sit down, Prince. Prince!

Now, where's that bloody alternator? Managed?

Oh any time, love. I'll not charge you for that

because it's nothing of a job. If you want

us again we're in the book. Tell your husband.

The poet is adopting a male persona. How would you describe him? Circle the words that best fit his persona from the following list.

> assertive   patronising   thoughtful   encouraging
>
> helpful   friendly   over-familiar   sexist
>
> disrespectful   offensive   considerate   teasing

Consider how the following quotations reveal the power situation:

a) 'don't panic', 'fetch', 'prop', 'go on', 'try and slide', 'create', 'push', 'fill', 'don't mind him', 'tell'

....

....

....

b) 'that's why', 'you see it's Russian', 'it's corrosive', 'rusts, you know'

....

....

....

c) 'and some soft roll above the cistern', 'he doesn't bite'

....

....

....

d) 'no clockwise', 'gently … and I mean gently'

....

....

....

Write two paragraphs showing how the male persona uses language to:

- address the woman
- describe tools, car parts and the topping-up process
- communicate with the woman after she has done the job.

_____

_____

_____

_____

_____

_____

_____

_____

_____

_____

_____

_____

Extend

Write a paragraph about the relationship between the title and the poem.

Active Learning

Imagine how the woman is feeling as she gets into her car and drives away from the garage. Write down her thoughts as a stream of consciousness.

Fill in the thought bubbles with what you think the woman mights be thinking.

GO ON, IT WON'T EAT YOU

OH DON'T MIND HIM LOVE, HE DOESN'T BITE

I'LL NOT CHARGE YOU FOR THAT BECAUSE...

'Being Boring' by Wendy Cope

'May you live in interesting times.' Chinese curse

If you ask me 'What's new?' I have nothing to say
Except that the garden is growing.
I have a slight cold but it's better today.
I'm content with the way things are going.
Yes, he is the same as he usually is,
Still eating and sleeping and snoring.
I get on with my work. He gets on with his.
I know this is all very boring.

There was drama enough in my turbulent past:
Tears and passion – I've used up a tankful.
No news is good news, and long may it last.
If nothing much happens, I'm thankful.
A happier cabbage you never did see,
My vegetable spirits are soaring.
If you're after excitement, steer well clear of me.
I want to go on being boring.

I don't go to parties. Well, what are they for,
If you don't want to find a new lover?
You drink and you listen and drink a bit more
And you take the next day to recover.
Someone to stay home with was all my desire
And, now that I've found a safe mooring,
I've just one ambition in life: I aspire
To go on and on being boring.

The poet is adopting a female persona. Circle the words that best fit her persona from the list below.

depressed	calm	resigned	accepting
realistic	witty	happy	funny
amusing	at ease	untroubled	fulfilled
satisfied	pessimistic		unworried

The poem has a strong sense of spoken voice.

a) How do the following quotations contribute to this effect?

> 'I'm content with the way things are going …'
>
> 'No news is good news, and long may it last.'
>
> 'If you're after excitement, steer well clear of me.'

....

....

b) What do the following quotations add to the voice?

> 'A happier cabbage …'
>
> 'My vegetable spirits …'

....

....

c) Identify the lines which sound as if the persona is:

(i) answering a question that her listener has posed

....

(ii) reacting to a comment or a non-verbal response made by her listener

....

(iii) confiding something to her listener.

....

What is revealed about the speaker during the poem? Make sure you refer to all three sections of the poem.

....

....

....

....

....

....

....

....

Extend

Write a paragraph which comments on the epigram ('*May you live in interesting times*'. Chinese curse) and the use of rhyme on the tone of the poem.

Active Learning

In what way is the tone of the poem both positive and negative? Make a learning poster to illustrate different aspects of the tone.

Complete the thought bubbles but, rather than using lines from the poem, think about what the female character might realistically be thinking before she has the time to reflect and find humour in her situation.

'The Sweet Menu' by Jeremy Hughes

I'm shown to a table for two,
The other chair is pulled back as if someone will come.

Families sit at the tables around me.
A baby in a high chair is being taught to clap,

A small boy digs in ice cream.
There is a flower in a bottle on my table.

There is water in the bottle but the flower is plastic.
A lily.

The chair facing me is beech.
The women who wait the table spin with trays of drinks and plates.

Apple juice and a mushroom pizza please.
The juice is cool,

The pizza hot and peppery.
The ceiling is made up of panels of glass

And everyone looks good in the light
The cold north wind has brought.

I eat and drink and face the chair.
The woman who looks after me pirouettes to my table.

I'd like to talk to someone about
The plastic lily in the bottle of water.

Would you like to see the sweet menu?
Facing me is the chair.

I'd like to spend time choosing,
This one or *That one*

But say
No thanks and ask for the bill.

I tip the woman who pliés with my receipt
and think, it hasn't come to much.

This poem makes use of the device of listing.

a) What types of things does the first-person narrator notice?

....

....

....

b) What effect does the listing have on the mood of the poem?

....

....

....

Revise 2

What do the following quotations communicate about the narrator's thoughts and feelings?

a) 'The other chair is pulled back as if someone will come.'

....

....

....

b) 'I eat and drink and face the chair.'

....

....

....

c) 'I'd like to talk to someone about / the plastic lily ...'

'I'd like to spend time choosing.'

....

....

....

....

....

There are short pieces of dialogue in the poem. What does the dialogue convey and how does it affect your response to the first-person narrator?

_____

_____

_____

_____

_____

_____

_____

_____

_____

_____

_____

_____

_____

_____

_____

_____

Extend

Write a paragraph about your response to the first-person narrator and the environment he is in. Include a comment about the final line.

Active Learning

Make a collage to reflect the many images in the poem. If you can't find a suitable image, then sketch your own. You could also try and write your own poem using the device of listing. The form that the poet uses here – two line stanzas – could be used as a structure.

'Tamer and Hawk' by Thom Gunn

I thought I was so tough

But gentled at your hands

Cannot be quick enough

To fly for you and show

That when I go I go

At your commands.

Even in the flight above

I am no longer free:

You seeled[1] me with your love,

I am blind to other birds –

The habit of your words

Has hooded me.

As formerly I wheel

I hover and twist,

But only want the feel

In my possessive thought,

Of catcher and caught

Upon your wrist.

You but half-civilise,

Taming me in this way.

Through having only eyes

For you I fear to lose,

I lose to keep, and choose

Tamer as prey.

[1]a falconry term from the verb 'to seel' meaning to sew up the eyelids of a hawk so it becomes quiet and easier to train

a) How would you describe the hawk? Circle the words that best fit the persona from the list below.

happy	sad	wanting to please	obedient	trapped	tamed

domesticated   menacing   predatory   loving   vulnerable

b) Select quotations that communicate mood and tone by conveying the following feelings or attitudes:

   (i)   Sadness

    ....

   (ii)   Respect for the tamer

    ....

   (iii) Superiority over the tamer

    ....

   (iv) Implicit criticism of the tamer

    ....

   (v)   Love for the tamer

    ....

   (vi) Vulnerability

    ....

   (vii) Threat

    ....

The poet uses a metaphor, comparing hawk and tamer to two lovers in an unequal relationship. Identify some lines which describe love as:

a) having the power to change someone's nature

....

b) a loss of freedom

....

c) a desire to please

....

d) blind

....

e) cruel

....

f) obsessive

....

This poem tells a story about the relationship between hawk and tamer from the hawk's perspective. For each stanza, write a sentence about how the story develops.

Stanza 1:

....

....

....

....

Stanza 2:

....

....

....

....

Stanza 3:

....

....

....

....

Stanza 4:

....

....

....

....

....

Extend

Write a paragraph on the rhyme and metre and its relationship to the poem's subject matter.

Active Learning

Find out about the sport of falconry and what is involved in training and keeping a hawk. Make a learning poster and annotate it with lines from the poem.

'The night is darkening round me' by Emily Brontë

The night is darkening round me

The wild winds coldly blow;

But a tyrant spell has bound me,

And I cannot, cannot go.

The giant trees are bending

Their bare boughs weighed with snow;

The storm is fast descending,

And yet I cannot go.

Clouds beyond clouds above me,

Wastes[1] beyond wastes below;

But nothing drear[2] can move me;

I will not, cannot go.

[1]a large area of uninhabited space; [2]dreary, dull and bleak

---

> ## Revise 1

a) Circle the adjectives that best describe the poem's setting:

strange	haunting	sad	exposed
bleak	desolate	unruly	nightmarish
wintry	realistic	elemental	terrifying
	isolated	unpeopled	oppressive

b) Write two sentences about the setting using one or more of the words you circled. Embed a quotation in one of your sentences.

_____

_____

_____

_____

_____

_____

c) Read these statements about the speaker's relationship to the setting. Link the statements to particular lines in the poem.

    (i) the speaker is spellbound

       ....

    (ii) the speaker is oppressed

       ....

    (iii) the speaker is suspended

       ....

    (iv) the speaker wants to go but can't

       ....

    (v) the speaker decides to stay

       ....

> **Revise 2**

a) What do you notice about the rhyme scheme? Use letters to mark out the pattern. How does the rhyme scheme add to the emotional feel/mood of the poem?

....

....

....

b) Explore the metre. How many syllables are there in each line? Is there a dominant stress pattern?

....

....

....

c) Can you find lines that break the stress pattern? How and where do they break it? What effect do they have on the meaning?

....

....

....

....

d) What other sound patterns do you notice besides rhyme? What effect do these sound patterns have on meaning?

....

....

....

....

Write about the structural patterning of the poem. Refer to the number of sentences, the punctuation of the sentences and the narrative structure of each of the three quatrains.

_____
_____
_____
_____
_____
_____
_____
_____
_____
_____
_____
_____
_____
_____
_____
_____
_____
_____
_____
_____
_____

Extend

How does the speaker's description of the setting suggest her emotional state? Write a paragraph.

Active Learning

Find out how the literary concept of 'the gothic' applies to this poem. Make a poster to record your findings and to display relevant 'gothic' images. Anchor the images with lines from the poem.

'Twice Shy' by Seamus Heaney

Her scarf à la Bardot[1],

In suede flats for the walk,

She came with me one evening

For air and friendly talk.

We crossed the quiet river,

Took the embankment walk.

Traffic holding its breath,

Sky a tense diaphragm:

Dusk hung like a backcloth

That shook where a swan swam

Tremulous as a hawk

Hanging deadly, calm.

A vacuum of need

Collapsed each hunting heart

But tremulously we held

As hawk and prey apart,

Preserved classic decorum[2],

Deployed our talk with art.

Our Juvenilia[3]

Had taught us both to wait,

Not to publish feeling

And regret it all too late –

Mushroom loves already

Had puffed and burst in hate.

So chary[4] and excited,

As a thrush linked on a hawk,

We thrilled to the March twilight

With nervous childish talk:

Still waters running deep

Along the embankment walk.

[1]in the style of Brigitte Bardot, a French actress and singer, popular in the mid-20th century and an icon of popular culture; [2]behaving with good taste and decency; [3]youth; [4]watchful or guarded

Revise 1

This poem tells the story of a romantic embankment walk. The speaker is a young man, probably a teenager. The poet uses the external environment to reflect the speaker's internal feelings and thoughts. Identify examples of:

a) suspense and anticipation

b) shyness, nervousness and uncertainty

c) caution and reluctance to communicate openly

a) hidden passion

Revise 2

The poet uses a variety of imagery throughout the poem. Similes, metaphors and personification are used to set the scene, build mood and express feelings. The two young people are compared to aspects of the natural world. Choose three of the following images and explore their meaning and how they are used.

a) Traffic holding its breath **b)** Sky a tense diaphragm **c)** Dusk hung like a backcloth **d)** As hawk and prey apart **e)** Mushroom loves already had puffcd and burst in hate **f)** As a thrush linked on a hawk **g)** Still waters running deep

Think about the title of the poem. What does the phrase 'Twice Shy' remind you of? Write a paragraph explaining how an understanding of the title affects your interpretation of the poem.

Extend

Look closely at the opening and closing stanzas. Think about how the poem opens and closes. Write two paragraphs.

Active Learning

Create a collage to reflect some of the images conveyed in the poem. Anchor the images with lines from the poem.

Patterns of Sound and Sense

'Travel' by Edna St Vincent Millay

The railroad track is miles away

And the day is loud with voices speaking.

Yet there isn't a train goes by all day

But I hear its whistle shrieking.

All night there isn't a train go by,

Though the night is still for sleep and dreaming,

But I see its wonders red on the sky,

And I hear its engine steaming.

My heart is warm with the friends I make,

And better friends I'll not be knowing;

Yet there isn't a train I wouldn't take,

No matter where it's going.

Revise 1

a) What do you notice about the rhyme scheme? Use letters to mark out the pattern.

b) What do you notice about the effect of rhyme and rhythm and their relationship to the poem's subject matter?

The poem is organised into three quatrains. Each quatrain is an exploration of the speaker's thoughts/perceptions. Each line in the quatrain has a role to play in creating meaning. Explain the purposes of the first, second, third and fourth lines of each quatrain.

Revise 3

What does the third quatrain reveal about the speaker? Write a paragraph.

Extend

What is the effect of the repetition of the statement 'there isn't a train' in each quatrain? Write a paragraph.

Active Learning

Look at this image of an American steam train. How do you respond to the idea of train travel? Write a creative response.

'Quiet Zone' by Roger McGough

(Poem for a lady on the Bristol to Paddington train, who spent the journey in the 'Quiet Coach', chatting on her mobile phone.)

With respect, this is the quiet zone.

And although when travelling on your own

it's nice to have a good old chat

with someone on the phone

This is the quiet zone.

'Shhh ... Quiet!' say the signs

on every table, window and door

obviously nothing to do with mobiles

so what do you think they're for?

A warning perhaps to brass bands

looking for a place to rehearse?

To the horde of angry soccer fans

who need to stamp and curse?

A troop of soldiers on the march

tramp, tramp. Or worse?

A stampede of trumpeting elephants?

A disruptive class of kids?

The entire cast of Stomp[1] banging dustbin lids?

A volcano bursting to erupt?

An unexploded mine?

'Shhh ... Quiet!' With respect,

Can't you read the sign?

[1] a performance group that blends rhythm, movement and dance and uses everyday objects like bin lids and brooms as instruments

Revise 1

Underline some examples from the poem that make it sound like speech.

Revise 2

How would you describe the speaker's tone? Use the options that you think are the best fit to write a paragraph about the speaker's tone.

judgemental	angry	ironic	scornful	contemptuous	patronising
condescending	superior	humorous	amusing	disapproving	extreme
	playful	outraged	irritated		

Revise 3

The poem is divided into four sections of varying lengths. Why do you think the poet has structured the poem in this way?

Extend

What is the purpose of the words in italics under the title? How do they affect your understanding of the poem?

Active Learning

Imagine you are the woman, aware that you are being observed by the speaker of the poem. Write a creative response to the poem from her perspective.

In the examination, the Unseen Poetry section has two questions:

- The first question is on a single poem and is worth 24 marks.
- The second question asks you to compare and contrast the poem with another poem and is worth 8 marks.

As you have 45 minutes in total for the Unseen Poetry section, you should spend around 30 minutes on the first question and around 10 minutes on the second question, with five minutes to check your responses.

The following information and activities will help you prepare for the examination.

Bear in mind the Assessment Objectives below as you complete the activities.

Assessment Objectives

First Poem

AO1: Understand and respond to the poem (12 marks)

You should make a range of points in response to the question and the poem, supporting them with brief quotations or references, organising them logically, and writing in an appropriately formal style.

Lower (1–4 marks)	Middle (5–8 marks)	Upper (9–12 marks)
A relevant response with some explanation and some supporting references from the poem.	A clear, explained response to the question; effective use of references to support explanation.	A critical, exploratory response to the question and the poem; well-chosen, precise references to support interpretation(s).

AO2: Analyse effects of language, form and structure (12 marks)

You must analyse how word choices, language techniques, form and structure create meaning, using appropriate literary terminology (e.g. 'simile').

Lower (1–4 marks)	Middle (5–8 marks)	Upper (9–12 marks)
Identification of some poetic methods, with some comment on their effects, using some terminology.	A clear explanation of a range of poetic methods and their effects, using accurate terminology.	Insightful analysis of poetic methods and exploration of their effects, with a range of well-chosen and accurate terminology.

Comparison Question

This question does not assess AO1. AO2 is assessed as for the main question, except that you will need to make comparisons and will not be expected to go into so much detail.

Lower (1–4 marks)	Middle (5–6 marks)	Upper (7–8 marks)
Some links between poets' use of language, structure or form and their effects on the reader. At the top of this level, links will be more relevant and there will be some comparison of the effects of poets' methods to create meaning.	A thoughtful comparison of poets' use of language, and/or structure, and/or form, and their effects; terminology used effectively to support analysis.	An exploratory and convincing comparison of poets' use of language, structure and form, and their effects; well-chosen terminology used effectively.

Reading the Question and Annotating the Poem

- Read the question and underline the key words.

- Read the poem carefully with the question in mind, and try to get a sense of the content.

- Annotate the poem as you re-read it. There will be certain lines that draw you in, so make sure you explore them.

- Select some methods to focus on: how mood/tone is created; the use/effect of particular words or phrases (e.g. to describe a character/scene or set a mood, to add a sense of realism or mystery); structural elements (how the poem is organised); patterns of words; patterns of sounds; imagery; titles (sometimes helpful in signalling the content of the poem); tense; punctuation. You don't have to write about every detail, so select the methods that catch your attention and are important for the poem's meaning.

Sample Annotations

Read the following poem and the sample annotations.

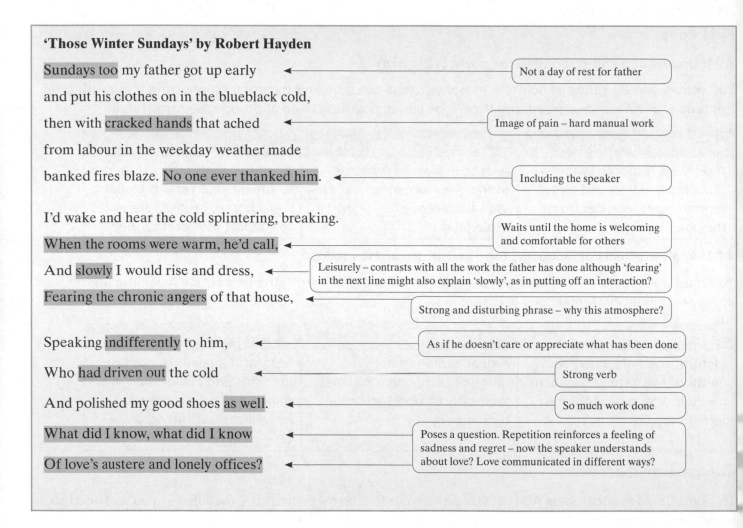

'Those Winter Sundays' by Robert Hayden

Sundays too my father got up early → Not a day of rest for father

and put his clothes on in the blueblack cold,

then with cracked hands that ached → Image of pain – hard manual work

from labour in the weekday weather made

banked fires blaze. No one ever thanked him. → Including the speaker

I'd wake and hear the cold splintering, breaking.

When the rooms were warm, he'd call, → Waits until the home is welcoming and comfortable for others

And slowly I would rise and dress, → Leisurely – contrasts with all the work the father has done although 'fearing' in the next line might also explain 'slowly', as in putting off an interaction?

Fearing the chronic angers of that house, → Strong and disturbing phrase – why this atmosphere?

Speaking indifferently to him, → As if he doesn't care or appreciate what has been done

Who had driven out the cold → Strong verb

And polished my good shoes as well. → So much work done

What did I know, what did I know → Poses a question. Repetition reinforces a feeling of sadness and regret – now the speaker understands about love? Love communicated in different ways?

Of love's austere and lonely offices?

Planning the Response

- Manage your time carefully.

- Make a quick plan for what you will include in the introduction, the three or four body paragraphs and the conclusion of your essay.

- Give yourself at least 20 minutes to write the essay.

Sample Plan: Response to a Single Poem

Question: How does the poet present the speaker's feelings about the father in 'Those Winter Sundays'? [24 marks]

Introduction: Perspective: son looking back. Negative feelings about self and attitude to father.

Para 1: Stanza 1: Opening sets tone – not a day of rest for father. Image 'cracked hands …' – hard work. 'No one ever … ' – explore meaning.

Para 2: Stanza 2: Use of 'I'd' – habitual past action. Details suggest the father's care. 'Chronic angers' – unexplained. Why this atmosphere?

Para 3: Stanza 3: Feelings of guilt. 'Indifferently'. Verbs 'driven out', 'polished'. Repetition 'What did …' and effect. Now speaker understands.

Conclusion: It's all about feelings. With time and experience comes understanding.

Writing the Introduction

- Try to communicate an overview of the poem.

- Make sure that you focus on the key words in the question.

> **Revise 1**
>
> Annotate the following sample introduction. Does it have an overview? Does it address the key words in the question?
>
> > The poet uses the perspective of a son looking back on his childhood and remembering the work his father did in the home, on winter Sundays as well as during the week. The feelings presented about the hardworking father are all tinged with negativity: sadness, regret and guilt.

Writing the Body of the Essay

- Start the main body of the essay with a paragraph about an important method used by the writer that links to the focus of the essay ('feelings about the father').

- Make sure that the topic sentences (the first sentence in each paragraph) focus on 'feelings about the father'.

- Make sure that you use some of the terms from the 'methods' list at the top of the previous page.

> **Revise 2**
>
> Annotate the sample body below. Think about the following:
>
> - Is the first paragraph making an important point?
> - Do all three paragraphs begin with a topic sentence?
> - Can you identify some methods the writer has used?
> - Are the writer's methods clearly linked to meaning?
> - Are the points made rooted in the text? Are quotations embedded?

The opening lines establish a subdued tone and mood, generated by the feelings expressed about the father. 'Sundays too …' implies that the speaker's father worked to support and care for his family on Sundays as on every other day. The striking image of soreness and the effects of hard manual 'labour' in the father's 'cracked hands' is linked, through assonance, with the image of 'banked fires blaze'. The power of this second image is enhanced by the strong /b/ alliteration. The speaker is quietly and sadly acknowledging his father's efforts. The closing statement of the first stanza, 'No one ever thanked him', is an admission of guilt because the speaker includes himself.

The speaker's feelings about his father are bound up with his behaviour as a child and the home atmosphere. The past tense 'I'd wake' reinforces the idea of looking back, but also suggests habitual actions, what the speaker 'would' regularly do. The descriptive language is quite simple, such as the speaker getting up 'slowly' once the house has warmed up. His leisurely behaviour contrasts with the father's purposeful activity. The descriptive language in 'fearing the chronic angers of the house' is more complex as it is unexplained and out of place with the fire's warmth. A negative mood persists, unattached to an individual.

The final stanza foregrounds the negative feelings attached to the speaker's relationship with the father. The adverb 'indifferently' describes the speaker's manner which he now regrets. The physical force implied in 'driven out the cold' and the afterthought of the polishing of 'my good shoes as well' echoes the meaning of 'too' at the start of the poem, emphasising the amount of work the father did for the family and the speaker in particular. The poem concludes with an emotional repeated question, 'What did I know, what did I know …?' The speaker's tone here is one of regret and sadness.

Writing the Conclusion

- Avoid repeating the key points from the body of the essay.
- Show some engagement with the poem's meaning.

Revise 3

Annotate the sample conclusion below. Does it avoid repeating the key points of the essay? Does it show some empathy and understanding of the poem?

> The feelings presented have a powerful emotional effect on the speaker and this transfers to the reader. The ending implies the speaker now understands that these 'offices' were acts of love. It makes the reader consider how love is understood and communicated and how time and experience help us to see life more clearly.

Extend

When you have read on and practised the skills of comparison and contrast, you might like to try this question:

In both 'Those Winter Sundays' and 'To My Nine-Year-Old Self' (page 25), the speakers describe the process of looking back to their younger self. What are the similarities and/or differences between the ways the poets present the process of looking back?

Question: In 'Composed on Westminster Bridge, September 3, 1802' how does the poet present the city of London? [24 marks]

Sample Annotations

Re-read the poem 'Composed on Westminster Bridge, September 3, 1802' and the sample annotations.

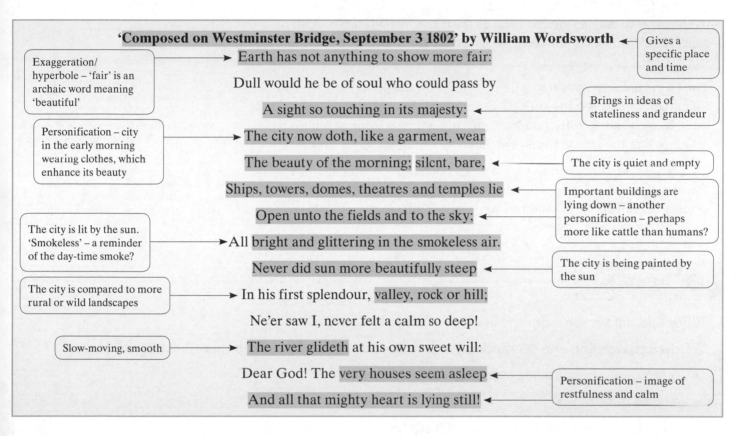

'Composed on Westminster Bridge, September 3 1802' by William Wordsworth — Gives a specific place and time

Earth has not anything to show more fair: — Exaggeration/hyperbole – 'fair' is an archaic word meaning 'beautiful'

Dull would he be of soul who could pass by

A sight so touching in its majesty: — Brings in ideas of stateliness and grandeur

The city now doth, like a garment, wear — Personification – city in the early morning wearing clothes, which enhance its beauty

The beauty of the morning; silent, bare, — The city is quiet and empty

Ships, towers, domes, theatres and temples lie — Important buildings are lying down – another personification – perhaps more like cattle than humans?

Open unto the fields and to the sky;

All bright and glittering in the smokeless air. — The city is lit by the sun. 'Smokeless' – a reminder of the day-time smoke?

Never did sun more beautifully steep — The city is being painted by the sun

In his first splendour, valley, rock or hill; — The city is compared to more rural or wild landscapes

Ne'er saw I, never felt a calm so deep!

The river glideth at his own sweet will: — Slow-moving, smooth

Dear God! The very houses seem asleep — Personification – image of restfulness and calm

And all that mighty heart is lying still!

Grade 5 Annotated Response

Read the following grade 5 sample response and annotations.

The poet uses the form of a Petrarchan sonnet to present London as a beautiful ('fair') and grand city. This beauty is partly because of the effect of the early morning sun[1] ('Never did sun more beautifully steep'). This is an image of the city being 'steeped' by the sun, like being painted by the light. 'Fair', 'beauty' and 'beautifully' all reinforce the speaker's pleasure in the city's appearance. Also, the adjectives 'bright' and 'glittering' reinforce the effects of the sunlight.[2]

1. Simple but effective comment that focuses on the question AO1

2. Some ability to focus on language and explain effects. Some useful brief quotations. Some ability to use terminology AO1 and AO2

The poet presents the city as a quiet place and the speaker feels 'a calm so deep!'. It is early morning before the city gets busy. The air is 'smokeless' and nobody is about on the streets.[3] The poet personifies the houses which 'seem asleep'. The river 'glideth at its own sweet will' is also personification, making the river sound as if it has a choice ('will').[4] 'Glideth' suggests a smooth movement. The ships are not moving. Words like 'silent' and 'bare' also create the same effect of quiet.[5]

The city has a relationship with nature.[6] Words like 'fields', 'sky', 'valley', 'rock' and 'hill' are used, which are all natural images.[7] The city appears to be close to countryside and this also reinforces the ideas of beauty, calm and quiet as the countryside is less busy than a city. The city is part of nature, which goes back to the idea of the sun's effect.

The city is also compared to a living being with the metaphor, 'And all that mighty heart is lying still!'. It has a 'heart' that will soon come to life.[8] 'Mighty' has positive connotations of power and almost sounds religious like the speaker is awe-struck.[9]

This is how the sonnet ends, on a note of wonder and exclamation. The city has had a deep spiritual effect on the speaker. Sonnets often express serious thoughts and feelings, like this one.[10]

> 3. Rather informal AO1

> 4. Two examples of personification noted with a little explanation AO2

> 5. The beginnings of some comment on language and meaning AO2

> 6. Point has potential but is rather vague AO1

> 7. The language needs more exploration AO2 AO1

> 8. Some explanation of the metaphor here AO2

> 9. Thoughtful analysis of word choice AO2

> 10. Some interpretation of mood, theme and form in the conclusion AO2

Revise 1

Choose a paragraph from the essay to improve. You can:

- change wording and sentencing to make the essay more fluent and sophisticated
- reorganise points to improve organisation
- embed quotations
- provide more detailed and insightful analysis
- use more subject terminology for the methods.

Grade 7+ Annotated Response

Read the following grade 7+ sample response and annotations.

The poet presents London as a city of great beauty and splendour using the form of the Petrarchan sonnet to express strong feeling. The octave describes London in the early morning in an objective way. The sestet describes the personal feelings of the speaker, indicated by the exclamations and the pronoun 'I'. It also includes more natural references than the octave. The rhyme scheme of a, b, b, a, a, b, b, a, c, d, c, d, c, d reveals how the sonnet is divided, with two distinctive sets of rhyme.[1]

> 1. Effective introduction, commenting on both form and structure AO1, AO2

The sonnet establishes the main theme in its opening line. It is a bold statement about the beauty of the city, which is then developed in the rest of the octave. The first-person speaker states that someone unable to appreciate London's beauty would be 'dull', in some way lacking in understanding and perception. 'A sight so touching' signals the argument of the sestet – the power to be moved by beauty.[2]

> 2. Clear understanding of the poem with a clear focus on theme and tone and use of precise references AO1, AO2

The poet effectively uses a number of literary devices in his presentation of the city. The simile in 'This city now doth, like a garment, wear …' develops the idea of London being dressed like royalty, which was introduced by the abstract noun 'majesty' used to suggest the city's grandeur. This serves to personify London and give it a grace, echoed in the stately pace of the iambic pentameter. The city is presented as a place of culture with its 'towers, domes, theatres and temples' and these details also suggest the panoramic nature of the view. The image of the buildings 'open unto the fields' also presents the city in harmony with nature.[3]

> 3. Very good range of terminology AO2

The sestet begins with a non-iambic foot 'NEVer did sun more beautifully steep', which has an emphasis on the first syllable. This draws attention to the word and the idea it expresses, emphasising the city's beauty. The speaker confidently asserts that the sunrise enhances the city with as much or more intensity as it would a natural feature such as a 'valley, rock or hill'. Also the use of the verb 'steep' suggests a painter's eye, drawn to the effects of the sunlight. This links back to the first word of the poem's title, 'composed'.[4]

> 4. Links form, features and effects AO2

The sonnet closes with a build-up of personal feelings. The speaker refers to 'a calm so deep' and the exclamatory 'Dear God!' has a strong expressive effect. The rhyming words 'deep' and 'asleep' are linked by form and meaning. It is as if the restfulness of the city has been transferred to the speaker. The final line concludes the speaker's line of thinking, the metaphor of the 'mighty heart' providing a striking image of London's dormant power.[5]

> 5. A close exploration of the ending of the poem, with careful attention to presentational devices and embedded quotations AO2, AO1

The sonnet reflects on the experience of observing London in the early morning from the vantage point of Westminster Bridge. In describing the view and its profound effect on the first-person speaker, the poet makes this ordinary experience an extraordinary one.[6]

> 6. Effective conclusion, summing up the poem's impact, without repetition AO1

> **Revise 2**
>
> Re-read the grade 5 and grade 7+ responses. Write a paragraph explaining why the 7+ response deserves the higher grade. Think about organisation; fluency, including use of link words; level of analysis; use of quotations; and use of subject terminology for the methods.

Question: Both 'Composed on Westminster Bridge, September 3, 1802' and 'A London Thoroughfare. 2am' express feelings about London. What are the similarities and/or differences between the ways the poets describe these feelings? [8 marks]

Sample Annotations

Read the following poem and the sample annotations.

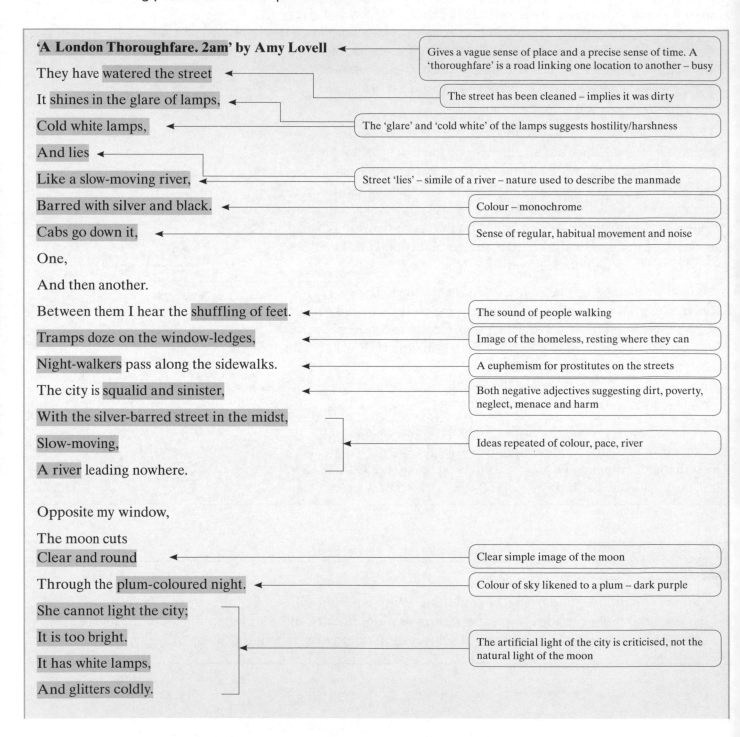

'A London Thoroughfare. 2am' by Amy Lovell

They have watered the street

It shines in the glare of lamps,

Cold white lamps,

And lies

Like a slow-moving river,

Barred with silver and black.

Cabs go down it,

One,

And then another.

Between them I hear the shuffling of feet.

Tramps doze on the window-ledges,

Night-walkers pass along the sidewalks.

The city is squalid and sinister,

With the silver-barred street in the midst,

Slow-moving,

A river leading nowhere.

Opposite my window,

The moon cuts
Clear and round

Through the plum-coloured night.

She cannot light the city;

It is too bright.

It has white lamps,

And glitters coldly.

Annotations:

- Gives a vague sense of place and a precise sense of time. A 'thoroughfare' is a road linking one location to another – busy
- The street has been cleaned – implies it was dirty
- The 'glare' and 'cold white' of the lamps suggests hostility/harshness
- Street 'lies' – simile of a river – nature used to describe the manmade
- Colour – monochrome
- Sense of regular, habitual movement and noise
- The sound of people walking
- Image of the homeless, resting where they can
- A euphemism for prostitutes on the streets
- Both negative adjectives suggesting dirt, poverty, neglect, menace and harm
- Ideas repeated of colour, pace, river
- Clear simple image of the moon
- Colour of sky likened to a plum – dark purple
- The artificial light of the city is criticised, not the natural light of the moon

I stand in the window and watch the moon.

She is thin and lustreless,

But I love her.

I know the moon,

And this is an alien city.

> 'Alien' suggests that the speaker does not know/ understand/come from London – in contrast to her familiarity with the moon

Grade 5 Sample Response

Read the following grade 5 sample comparative essay and annotations.

Both poems are about people's feelings when looking at London.[1] The first is full of praise. The second is full of dread. Speaker one loves London because of its 'beauty'. Speaker two hates London as it feels 'alien'. Wordsworth makes London sound 'bright' and appealing. Lowell makes London sound like a prison, 'cold' and 'barred.'[2]

> 1. Effective introductory sentence

> 2. Some comparisons drawn but more detail required

The imagery is very different. Wordsworth describes London as grand, wearing 'the beauty of the morning'. Lowell uses the words 'squalid and sinister', 'tramps' and 'night-walkers'. Wordsworth, however, mentions no people. There is a positive/negative contrast between the light imagery. Wordsworth's London is 'all bright and glittering' but Lowell makes the lamplight 'glare' 'cold' and 'white'. This imagery reflects positive and negative feelings.[3]

> 3. Looks more closely at imagery in this paragraph and draws some contrasts

The poems have a similar structure, first the city is described and then the speakers' feelings. Descriptions and feelings are linked. In Wordsworth's poem the final feelings are exclamations, expressing awe. Lowell uses repetition of 'cold', 'coldly' and 'white' to emphasise alienation. The only positive feeling communicated is 'love' for the moon.[4]

> 4. Brief comparison of structure

Both poets describe intense feelings but do so differently. Wordsworth's speaker is uplifted as the exclamations illustrate. Lowell's speaker sounds anxious.[5]

> 5. Brief conclusion

Revise 1

a) What strengths and weaknesses does this essay have? List them below.

....

....

....

b) Choose a paragraph to improve and rewrite it. You could:

- change wording and sentence types to make the essay more fluent
- use link words to add fluency
- provide a more insightful analysis
- use more subject terminology for the methods.

Grade 7+ Sample Response

Read the following grade 7+ sample comparative essay and annotations.

Both poets use pathetic fallacy to show the emotional effect London has on the speakers' feelings. Wordsworth's poem describes the speaker's vantage point from Westminster Bridge, where London is seen at sunrise in all its glory. This serves to elevate the feelings of the speaker, who implies that a person unable to appreciate such beauty must be 'dull'. Lowell's poem reflects the speaker's detachment as they look out of their window and down onto the 'alien city'. The use of the noun 'sidewalks' suggests the speaker is American and this would help explain the strong feeling of the outsider.[1]

> 1. Highly effective introduction focusing on a literary device used to different effect

Both poets use figurative language to animate London, giving it human qualities which affect the speakers' feelings, positively and negatively. Wordsworth's simile 'like a garment' and metaphor 'mighty heart' suggest London's dignity and energy, whereas Lowell's metaphors 'the glare of lamps' and 'glitters coldly' suggest hostility.[2]

> 2. Insightful contrast

The language used more generally in the poems reinforces the positive and negative feelings communicated. Wordsworth's poem contains a lexical set associated with a monarch's ceremonial dress to create feelings of awe ('majesty', 'garment', 'bright' and 'glittering'). Lowell's poem contains words that make the speaker sound critical: 'thin', 'lustreless', 'too bright' and 'a river leading nowhere'. These also reflect the speaker's negative mindset.[3]

> 3. Effective comparative analysis developing into an interpretation

Although both poems express intense first-person feelings, Wordsworth's Petrarchan sonnet sounds like speech whereas Lowell's poem sounds more like thought. This suits the subject matter. Wordsworth romanticises London and this is evident in the hyperbole, 'Ne'er saw I, never felt a calm so deep!'. Lowell's poem has more realism. It is a series of statements that describe what is seen and although it refers to 'a London thoroughfare', the feeling it generates is that there are many others like it. The positive simple statements expressing the speaker's feelings about the moon, 'I love her' and 'I know her', stand out from the other negative observations about the city. The idea that London is not known and therefore not loved is implicit. The brooding quality of the second poem sounds more private and contained than the first poem and more like unspoken thought.[4]

> 4. Effective analysis and accurate use of terminology

Revise 2

Re-read the grade 5 and grade 7+ responses. Write a paragraph explaining what makes the 7+ response better than the 5 response. Think about: organisation, fluency, level of analysis and use of subject terminology.

Exploring the First Poem

If 'Blackbird' by John Drinkwater were the first poem to be explored in the exam, the question might be: 'How does the poet present the blackbird?'

Sample Annotations

Read the following poem and the sample annotations.

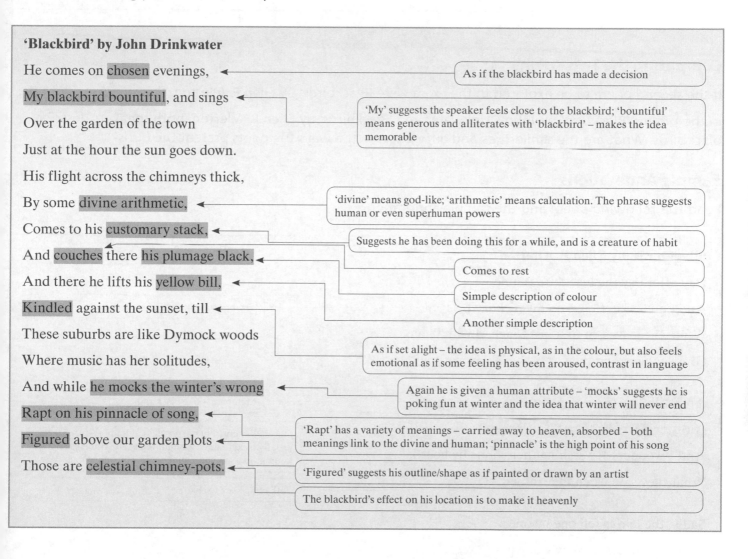

'Blackbird' by John Drinkwater

He comes on chosen evenings, ◄—— As if the blackbird has made a decision

My blackbird bountiful, and sings ◄—— 'My' suggests the speaker feels close to the blackbird; 'bountiful' means generous and alliterates with 'blackbird' – makes the idea memorable

Over the garden of the town

Just at the hour the sun goes down.

His flight across the chimneys thick,

By some divine arithmetic, ◄—— 'divine' means god-like; 'arithmetic' means calculation. The phrase suggests human or even superhuman powers

Comes to his customary stack, ◄—— Suggests he has been doing this for a while, and is a creature of habit

And couches there his plumage black, ◄—— Comes to rest

And there he lifts his yellow bill, ◄—— Simple description of colour

Kindled against the sunset, till ◄—— Another simple description

These suburbs are like Dymock woods

Where music has her solitudes, ◄—— As if set alight – the idea is physical, as in the colour, but also feels emotional as if some feeling has been aroused, contrast in language

And while he mocks the winter's wrong ◄—— Again he is given a human attribute – 'mocks' suggests he is poking fun at winter and the idea that winter will never end

Rapt on his pinnacle of song, ◄—— 'Rapt' has a variety of meanings – carried away to heaven, absorbed – both meanings link to the divine and human; 'pinnacle' is the high point of his song

Figured above our garden plots ◄—— 'Figured' suggests his outline/shape as if painted or drawn by an artist

Those are celestial chimney-pots. ◄—— The blackbird's effect on his location is to make it heavenly

Answer these questions on how the poet presents the blackbird. Include quotations to support your answers.

a) How is the blackbird described at the beginning of the poem?

b) Whereabouts is the blackbird? What is the setting of the poem?

c) How is the blackbird's appearance described during the course of the poem?

d) What type of image of the blackbird does the poet use to close the poem?

Comparing the Two Poems

If the second poem to be explored in the exam were 'Blackbirds' by Ellen P. Allerton, the question might be:

In the poems 'Blackbird' by John Drinkwater and 'Blackbirds' by Ellen P. Allerton, both speakers describe blackbirds. What are the similarities and differences in the ways the poets present the birds?

Sample Annotations

Read the following poem and the sample annotations.

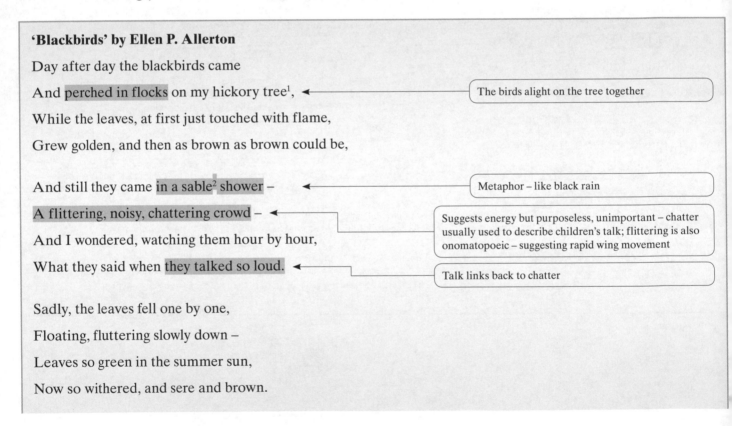

'Blackbirds' by Ellen P. Allerton

Day after day the blackbirds came

And perched in flocks on my hickory tree[1], ◄——— The birds alight on the tree together

While the leaves, at first just touched with flame,

Grew golden, and then as brown as brown could be,

And still they came in a sable[2] shower – ◄——— Metaphor – like black rain

A flittering, noisy, chattering crowd – ◄——— Suggests energy but purposeless, unimportant – chatter usually used to describe children's talk; flittering is also onomatopoeic – suggesting rapid wing movement

And I wondered, watching them hour by hour,

What they said when they talked so loud. ◄——— Talk links back to chatter

Sadly, the leaves fell one by one,

Floating, fluttering slowly down –

Leaves so green in the summer sun,

Now so withered, and sere and brown.

The trees are bare: I watched one day

In vain – the blackbirds came no more; ← **Their absence**

And then I knew they had fled away, ← **Idea of running away from danger**

And my sorrowful thought this burden bore:

The winds shall blow through my hickory tree,

The sifting snow and the sleety rain:

But, little I know what awaiteth me

Ere the leaves and the blackbirds come again! ← **Sense of their return being knowable, creatures of habit**

[1]the hickory tree belongs to the walnut tree family and is found in North America; [2]sable means black or very dark brown

Revise 2

Answer these questions on how the poet presents the blackbirds. Include quotations to support your answers.

a) At the beginning, how does the poet present the group of blackbirds?

b) Whereabouts are the blackbirds? What is the setting of the poem?

c) What is the blackbirds' appearance compared to during the course of the poem?

d) How do the blackbirds behave and to whom are they compared?

e) Describe the effect of the two metaphors.

Revise 3

Create a table and make a note of some key similarities and differences between the two poems. Focus on: the appearance, behaviour and sound of the blackbirds; the effect of the blackbirds on the speakers; and the methods used to present the blackbirds.

Comparing the Poems

Comparison Method 1

For this method, you write one or more paragraphs on the similarities and one or more paragraphs on the differences. Here is an example.

Revise 4

Underline the words that are used to indicate where similarities and differences are being written about.

Similarities

Both poems use personification as a descriptive device. In the first poem, the words 'chosen' and 'bountiful' give the blackbird qualities of decision making and generosity. Similarly, the second poem uses 'chattering' and 'talked' to suggest the blackbirds' human-like communication. The use of personification in both poems helps to give the blackbirds a character.

The poems also share another similarity in that they both make use of the first-person speaker whose observation of the blackbirds leads to an emotional response. In the first poem, the phrase 'my blackbird' conveys personal affection. In the second poem, the speaker watches the blackbirds 'hour by hour' and associates their absence with a lack of knowledge, 'little I know what awaiteth me'.

Differences

The use of colour to describe the appearance of the blackbirds is different. In the first poem, the colours 'black' and 'yellow' are simple and straightforward, whereas in the second poem the colour is more unusual. 'Sable' suggests both dark brown and black and also the soft texture of fur from the animal of the same name.

Another contrast is how frequently the blackbirds visit. In the first poem, the blackbird comes on 'chosen evenings'. His appearance is less predictable than the blackbirds of the second poem who come 'day after day'. This difference is important for the meaning of the poems. The less frequent appearance of the blackbird in the first poem makes his visits 'bountiful', like a gift. The regularity of the blackbirds' presence in the second poem creates an expectation and their absence generates a 'sorrowful thought'.

Comparison Method 2

For this method, you include similarities and differences within the same paragraph. This is an integrated approach.

Revise 5

Underline the words that are used to indicate where similarities and differences are being written about.

Both poems share similar subject matter as they are about blackbirds. The first poem focuses on a solitary blackbird, referred to as 'he', but the second focuses on a group, described as both a 'flock' and a 'crowd'. The blackbird of the first poem is individualised whereas the 'noisy' 'chattering' blackbirds of the second poem are not, as they all behave in the same way.

The Language of Comparison and Contrast

When you make comparisons and contrasts, whichever method you prefer, you will need to signal the similarities and differences. There are several helpful words/phrases that will help you to organise your writing.

Revise 6

Look at the following words and phrases. Identify whether each word or phrase signals a similarity or a difference.

on the other hand	similarly	in contrast	despite these similarities
however	likewise	whereas	also	in the same way	conversely
both	despite these differences	even though	along the same lines

Similarities:

_____

_____

Differences:

_____

_____

Writing an Introduction for the Comparative Essay

The introduction needs to engage with the focus of the question (i.e. the presentation of the blackbirds) and establish some key points of similarity and difference about the two poems.

Revise 7

Read the following sample introduction and make annotations on:

- how the qualities of each poem are introduced
- how comparisons/contrasts are introduced.

> The first poem presents a positive image of the solitary male blackbird who appears on 'chosen evenings'. In the suburban setting, with its 'chimneys thick', his presence feels 'bountiful', like a personal gift to the speaker. In the second poem, a 'crowd' of blackbirds are presented in the 'hickory tree' of the speaker's garden, which feels more isolated and rural. The presentation of these blackbirds is also positive, but their absence at the end is associated with sadness. Both speakers are affected by the birds and this gives the poems their emotional power.

Comparing Mood and Voice

Ask yourself:

- What emotions are generated to create the mood?
- What characterises the speakers' voices?
- What attitudes are conveyed towards the blackbirds?
- Is there a dominant tone?
- Are there shifts in tone and mood or do they remain stable?

> **Revise 8**
>
> Choose your comparative method and write one or two paragraphs comparing the mood and voice of the poems.

Comparing Structure and Narrative

Ask yourself:

- Does each poem tell a story?
- Is the story about an event?
- Does the story make a point?
- Does the structure follow the narrative?

> **Revise 9**
>
> Choose your comparative method and write one or two paragraphs comparing structure and narrative.

Comparing Form

Ask yourself:

- Does each poem have a metre or rhyme scheme?
- If so, what is the effect?
- How is each poem organised?

> **Revise 10**
>
> Choose your comparative method and write one or two paragraphs comparing metre and rhyme.

Writing a Conclusion

A conclusion should not simply repeat the main points of the essay. It should aim to leave the reader with a view on the similarities and differences and a sense of personal engagement.

Read the two responses below, which are both conclusions to the essay. Annotate the responses. Write a paragraph explaining which one you think is better and why.

Sample 1 Conclusion

In conclusion, both poems present the blackbirds as behaving in a mysterious way. In the first poem, this mystery is combined with a religious type of wonder, whereas in the second the mystery is combined with personal sadness when the blackbirds leave. The line 'But, little I know what awaiteth me', towards the end of the second poem, expresses a universal fear about life's mysteries. The first poem implies that the mystery is connected with the 'divine' and would appeal to readers who share that belief. The second poem is easy to understand because of its language, structure and form; its message about what is known and not known about life would resonate with many readers, including myself.

Sample 2 Conclusion

In conclusion, there are many similarities and differences between the two poems. The appearance, sound and behaviour of the blackbirds are described in detail in both poems. The poems both include first-person speakers who are affected by the visits of the blackbirds, as has already been indicated in this essay. I prefer the first poem as I like the special one-to-one relationship between the speaker and the solitary blackbird. The second poem feels a bit old-fashioned with words like 'ere' and 'awaiteth' and appeals to me less. I also like the upbeat tone of the first poem whereas the second poem leaves me feeling a bit sad.

Answers

Pages 4–5

Revise 1 Answers might include: What is the subject matter of the poem? What is the mood of the poem? What feelings are communicated by the speaker? Are there any patterns of words that stand out? How is the poem organised? How does the poem end?

Revise 2 Father's actions: 'got up early', 'put his clothes on in the blueblack cold', 'made / banked fires blaze', 'he'd call', 'driven out the cold', 'polished my good shoes' **Speaker's actions/thoughts/feelings:** 'I'd wake and hear', 'slowly I would rise and dress', 'fearing the chronic angers', 'speaking indifferently to him', 'what did I know …'

Revise 3 a) Establishes a theme of hard work. **b)** Suggests the father's work was taken for granted by everybody, including the speaker. **c)** Signals the development of another theme, difficult family relations. **d)** Suggests a tense and hostile atmosphere at home. **e)** Reveals guilt on the speaker's part and relates back to the father's work being taken for granted.

Extend Sample answer: The father is presented as hardworking. He 'got up early' to do the chores and to make the home warm for his family by making the fires 'blaze'. He works alone and there is no mention of a wife. His solitary nature is also suggested through the reference to 'lonely offices' at the end. His actions are those of a protective father, seeing to his family's needs. 'Driven out the cold' suggests force and 'polished my good shoes' suggests a need for respectability. These actions appear to suggest fatherly love although this is only appreciated by the speaker as an adult.

The speaker presents himself as a child who has the freedom to get up later on a Sunday. 'I'd wake and hear' suggests a leisurely start to the day. 'Slowly I would rise and dress' reinforces this idea but 'fearing the chronic angers' adds a negative note of anticipation. He speaks 'indifferently' to his father, which reveals a lack of acknowledgement of his father's actions and a lack of concern for his feelings. The repetition of 'what did I know' suggests that the speaker now understands something about love which he did not do at the time.

Pages 6–8

Revise 1 Answers might include: **a)** 'All bright and glittering' **b)** 'Dull would he be of soul' **c)** 'A sight so touching' **d)** 'Never did sun more beautifully steep' **e)** 'Ne'er saw I, never felt a calm so deep!' **f)** 'The very houses seem asleep' **g)** 'Earth has not anything to show more fair'

Revise 2 Answers might include: **a)** The adjectives 'silent' and 'bare' both convey a sense of quiet through a lack of people. 'Open' conveys the stillness of an empty space. 'Lie' suggests a relaxed state. The pause between 'lie' and 'open' caused by the line break also slows down the pace. **b)** The verb 'glideth' conveys a sense of smooth and quiet motion. **c)** The use of 'asleep' suggests both quiet and stillness, as if the houses themselves, as well as their occupants, are at rest. The word 'still' means not moving and not making a sound. Both these meanings come in to play here.

Revise 3 Sample answer: The first eight lines convey a mood of contentment and a tone of admiration. The speaker's thoughts are conveyed as he looks at the city. The opening hyperbolic statement 'Earth has not anything to show more fair' establishes the speaker's positive attitude. The quiet challenge made to anyone who does not share the speaker's opinion ('dull would he be') does not disrupt the uplifted tone. The dignity of the city is conveyed through the abstract noun 'majesty' which maintains an elevated mood.

Personal feelings of wonder, awe and inner calm are expressed in the final six lines, which subtly change the mood and tone. The speaker sounds as if he has been changed by what he has seen. Exclamations such as 'Dear God!' make it sound as if these feelings have been spoken aloud. The repetition of 'ne'er' and 'never' also strengthens the tone of certainty felt by the speaker. There are echoes of the mood of quiet dignity established earlier (e.g. 'The river glideth at his own sweet will'), but the poem closes with a strong emphatic exclamation. The reader is left in no doubt about the profound effect the city has had on the speaker.

Extend Answers might include: **a)** The first-person perspective enables a personal and direct expression of inner thoughts, feelings and attitude, which colour the mood and tone. **b)** The setting affects mood and tone as it is early morning at sunrise when the city is quiet and still and can be seen in all its majesty. **c)** The imagery helps the reader to visualise the city in a particular way, foregrounding grandeur and brightness. **d)** The language conveys the mood and tone by providing a pattern of meanings relating to stillness, quiet and light.

Pages 9–11

Revise 1 a) brown, silver-sheened, green-and-copper, olive-green, orange, green and copper **b)** thick, silver-sheened, sunshine, shade, shadows, brightness, light, flashed up, sun-thickened, darkness, gleam, blurred reflections **c)** dozed, lay, suddenly, flicked, ran, out, came, flashed up, passed, received **d)** water, sunshine, reeds, pike, stems, pool, willows, bank

Revise 2 Answers might include: **a)** The pike is still, then moves suddenly and quickly and then slowly. The motion of its movement at the end of the poem is not clear from 'passed' but suggests regularity or steadiness. **b)** 'Dozed' and 'lay' give the pike human qualities as if resting/relaxing. 'Passed' suggests a move in a specific direction, as if the pike is aware. It also gives the pike a stately grandeur as if he is king of the pool. **c)** At the beginning, the pike is in the darkness, out of the sunlight and 'lost' as if invisible. This changes when its sudden movement catches the light and its colours are visible. At the end of the poem, the pike is 'a darkness and a gleam' as it moves away and can only just be seen. **d)** The description of the pike's colours is precise: the adjective 'copper' denotes a specific shade of reddish brown. The poet uses hyphenated words to build an exact visual picture, e.g. the 'olive-green' light of the water and the phrase 'green-and-copper' to suggest a quick burst of mixed colour. Later, the separate adjectives 'green and copper' suggest that both colours can be seen distinctly.

Revise 3 a) (i) silver-sheened, sunshine, shade, reeds, lost, shadows, stems, unnoticed, suddenly, brightness, flashed, sun-thickened, so, fish passed across, darkness, reflections, willows, opposite, received **(ii)** brown, water, sheened, sunshine, cool, shade, reeds, dozed, lay, unnoticed, green, brightness, came, through, so, pool, gleam, received **b)** The pattern of the long drawn-out vowels enhances the poem's visual qualities by reinforcing a sense of relaxation and drowsiness at the beginning and a sense of stateliness at the end.

Extend Answers might include: Words that inject a sense of drama and mystery include 'lost' and 'unnoticed' which suggest that the pike is hidden or not visible and a latent threat. The adverb 'suddenly' disrupts the calm. 'Received' at the end suggests the willows' reflections are given to the pike, rather like a gift. This adds a mysterious quality to the ending but, on a more literal level, it could also be interpreted as the pike being admitted to another hiding place.

Pages 12–14

Revise 1 a) a, b, a, b, c, d, c, d, e, f, e, f, g, g **b)** three **c)** the last two lines

Revise 2 a) (i) Changes direction **(ii)** Introduces **(iii)** Develops **(iv)** Develops **b) (i)** 'peopled places', 'roaring', 'human flood', 'the crowd', 'billowing sounds and faces' **(ii)** 'of one who stands fronting the waste', 'endless sands', 'like a lost gull in solitary flight', 'single is', 'none may share', 'each is alone', 'uncompanioned'

Revise 3 Sample answer: The first quatrain introduces the theme of loneliness by describing settings where it is possible to feel lonely in the company of others. The imagery, which helps the reader to visualise this idea, conveys discomfort and hostility. The streets are 'roaring', which suggests a deep, prolonged and wild sound, and is nightmarish in this context. This is followed by an image of a crowded room with 'billowing sounds and faces' conveying the idea of a large undulating mass of people, possibly dancing. Again, there is a dream-like, dizzying quality to the image. The comparison made to 'foreign music, overshrill and loud' is negative, suggesting high-pitched, piercing notes that are difficult to listen to.

The second quatrain develops the theme by describing settings where loneliness is felt when not in the company of others. The link between the first and second quatrain is one of contrast. The image of someone standing 'fronting the waste' calls to mind the vast, inhospitable nature of the sea and the 'cold sea-light' emphasises bleakness outside as well as within. The metaphor of a 'wisp of flesh' and the simile of the 'lost gull' enhance the sense of vulnerability and lostness that loneliness entails.

The third quatrain develops the argument of the second by extending the idea of loneliness to the state of being 'single' (as in not in a stable relationship with another person). The pairing of 'up-rising and down-lying' evokes the sad image of getting up and going to bed alone. The lack of opportunity for shared intimacy in times of 'conquest' or 'despair' leads to psychological and physical isolation.

Extend Sample answer: The rhyming couplet cancels out the ideas in the rest of the poem with the word 'yet' which signals a surprising contrast. The speaker now uses the first-person pronoun which injects the poem with a personal perspective on the theme. Up until this point, the speaker's approach has been objective, as seen in the repeated use of 'there is the …'. It is a surprising shift as the reader might assume that the lonely feelings described in such detail must have been experienced. The romantic image the reader is left with is of the speaker 'locked' in an embrace and 'bent' beneath a kiss, symbolising physical intimacy. This image and the feeling it conveys contrast with the earlier stark images and disturbed feelings. Another way of interpreting the final image is to see it as oppressive rather than romantic. The force implied by 'locked' and 'bent' can be seen as disturbing.

Pages 15–16

Revise 1 Answers might include: **a)** 'He was my North … for ever' **b)** 'For nothing now can ever come to any good.' **c)** 'Stop all the clocks … silence the pianos' **d)** 'Let aeroplanes … black cotton gloves' **e)** 'The stars are not wanted … pour away the ocean'

Revise 2 a) (i) stop, cut off, prevent, silence, bring out, put, put out, pack up, dismantle, pour away, sweep up **(ii)** 'let the mourners come. Let aeroplanes circle', 'Let the traffic policemen wear' **(iii)** 'my North … my song' **b)** Answers should include: The lists add imagery and tone to the story. The commands are full of images, some humorous and absurd. The requests express strength of feeling, with the speaker imagining grand public symbols of mourning to mark his personal grief.

The descriptions add a tone of pathos, revealing the raw feelings of the speaker.

Revise 3 Sample answer: The funeral scene is set in the first quatrain through a list of commands made by the speaker to his audience. Most of the commands have a negative meaning ('stop', 'cut off' and 'prevent'), but build up to the final command, 'bring out', and the first request, an invitation to the mourners.

The mixture of requests and commands in the second quatrain provides an insight into the speaker's feelings. He needs to see his feelings reflected in the world around him. The third quatrain marks a shift in focus. The speaker now thinks about his dead lover and uses the metaphors of a compass and time to show how much he meant to him. The stanza ends with an acknowledgement that love has not lasted; death has taken it away.

The fourth quatrain sums up his negative thoughts and feelings. It is a list of commands that reject the natural world and its beauty. The final line signals deep despair.

Extend Sample answer: The first quatrain introduces a sombre mood, fitting for a funeral, although the image of the dog with a 'juicy bone' provides some light relief. The second quatrain contains some absurd and exaggerated imagery, for example the skywriting 'he is dead' and the doves with 'crêpe bows'. The third quatrain contrasts with the second and is much more sad in tone. It introduces a note of pathos as the speaker thinks about his lover. This sad tone changes to one of negativity and despair in the fourth quatrain.

Pages 17–19

Revise 1 Answers may vary and there will be overlaps. **a)** 'his apron, / the leather black and tan', 'the smoke slow-turning from his mouth', 'the wind twisting his sideburns', 'three nails gritted between his teeth **b)** 'blessing himself', 'pitches', 'waits', 'careful not to look her in the eye', 'runs his hand', 'checking', 'folding … leans into …', 'catches', 'cups', 'bends', 'cutting', 'excavating', 'filing', 'branding', 'placing', 'gives her a slap', 'watches her' **c)** 'Blessing himself with his apron', 'in an apparition of smoke' **d)** 'careful not to look her in the eye', 'gives her a slap', 'his steel, biting at her heels'

Revise 2 Sample answer: The poet keeps the mare's femaleness firmly in mind by repeating the pronoun 'her' throughout when describing parts of her body. She is compared to a bride towards the end of the poem in the metaphor describing the farrier 'pinning the dress of the bride'. Once the poem has been read, the early image of the farrier 'blessing himself' and the mare being 'led' to the yard might also suggest the idea of a bride being accompanied/walked into a church where the priest is waiting. The line beginning 'She smells him …' uses the simple device of pronouns to remind the reader of the horse's femaleness and the farrier's maleness. Her sense of smell is acute and

she appears to recognise 'woodbine', 'metal and hoof', a mixture of the man himself and his occupation. The phrase 'awkward in her new shoes' can be interpreted differently: the mare's new shoes will take some getting used to, but there is also a suggestion of self-consciousness or embarrassment at being watched.

Revise 3 Sample answer: His apron, a form of heavy-duty protective clothing, is likened to the colour of a 'rain-beaten bay'. This compares him with an animal, a horse who has been exposed to harsh weather. This imagery continues in the description of 'the wind twisting his sideburns' where the farrier's facial hair is curled by the force of the wind. The final line, 'The sound of his steel, biting at her heels', melds man and nature: 'his steel' is now part of her, and not only that, it is 'biting' which suggests pain or aggression, like a dog 'biting her heels'.

Extend Sample answer: The farrier is presented in his workplace where he is in control. His actions are those of a skilful man. The poet describes the farrier's un-rushed preparations, with time for a cigarette while he waits. Even the way he 'pitches' the roll-up suggests a well-practised but casual gesture. The smoke is 'slow-turning' which reinforces his stillness. There is an air of quiet confidence in his behaviour. He knows how to handle the mare and is 'careful not to look her in the eye'. The comparison of the mare to a 'lintel' and a 'knackered car' suggests that he objectifies her. His movements are precise as he works on her hoof. The verbs 'excavating' and 'filing' are examples of his dexterity. There is also a delicate beauty to his work with its 'moon silver clippings', reinforced by the striking metaphor of him as 'romantic lead' in a play or a film. His masculinity, apparent from the beginning, is tempered by this imagery and the feminine 'seamstress' metaphor. At the end, he reasserts his masculinity as he 'gives her a slap and watches her leave'.

Pages 20–21

Revise 1 Sample answer: The poet presents the children with 'innocent faces clean' and 'innocent hands' which reinforces their purity as a group. Their youth makes them free from any sin. They are compared to the natural world: 'Thames' waters', 'flowers', 'lambs', 'mighty wind' and 'harmonious thunderings'. The metaphors and similes suggest harmony, beauty and strength, all qualities that form a pattern of positive meanings. The children's 'radiance' suggests a brightness which is literal, as they are young and happy, but also metaphorical. There are connotations of holiness suggested by 'radiance' and also by the metaphor of the lamb, a Christian symbol of suffering, triumph and gentleness.

Revise 2 a) the rhyme scheme is rhyming couplets – six different rhymes **b)** most lines have fourteen syllables although some have fifteen **c)** the pattern is 7 feet of unstressed and stressed syllables (The CHILDren

WALKing TWO and TWO, in RED and BLUE and GREEN), called iambic heptameter. The last line of the first quatrain disrupts the rhythm as the children 'flow' in through the cathedral doors.

Revise 3 Sample answer: The opening quatrain sets the scene, giving the time (Holy Thursday) and place (St Paul's Cathedral) and a general description of the characters attending the service (the 'innocent' children and the 'grey-haired beadles', a contrast of youth and age). The second quatrain comments specifically on the quantity of children, using 'multitude', its plural form 'multitudes' and the enumerator 'thousands' to convey the scale of the event. Similes and metaphors are used to describe the children's appearance and behaviour. The final stanza comments on the emotional power of the children's singing and closes with a command or a warning: 'Then cherish pity…'.

Extend Sample answer: The final line, about a need to feel and act on 'pity', appears to address both the 'aged men, wise guardians of the poor' as well as the reader. It stands out from the rest of the poem because it is no longer within the world of the story. It communicates a moral and humane message about the importance of feeling pity for others.

Pages 22–24

Revise 1 Answers should include: 'From across the party I watch you, / watching her'; 'Do my possessive eyes / imagine your silent messages?'; 'I have come to recognise this code'; 'my eyes burn into your back'; 'my insides shout with rage'; 'You turn and meet my accusing stare head on'; 'Her eyes follow yours, meet mine'

Revise 2 a) Answers should include: **(i)** suggests jealousy **(ii)** indicates a cynical attitude, based on mistrust **(iii)** suggests that the speaker sees this as a calculated advance on the girl's part; the verb 'turning on' could have a second implied meaning of sexual excitement **(iv)** reveals the power of the speaker's imagination, 'mesmerised' denotes a trance-like state and reinforces the earlier use of 'bewitching' **(v)** reveals the speaker's perception of the situation as a competition and her judgement of the other girl's level of interest in her boyfriend **(vi)** implies anger on the speaker's part, she feels that he should feel guilt **b)** The verbs 'recognise', 'predict' and 'know' and the phrase 'so well' reveal the speaker's familiarity with the situation. She has observed similar encounters in the past and appears to be long-suffering but not exactly a victim.

Revise 3 Sample answer: The dialogue conveys a sense of ambiguity. The boy's words 'I'm bored' attempt to cover up and dismiss what has happened while also signalling his desire to leave the party, as if the fun is over. The fact that the speaker appears to accept her boyfriend's words at face value reinforces her passivity, suggested earlier in the words 'And there is nothing I can do'. Her acknowledgement of the other girl on departure with the informal 'bye'

said 'frostily' appears to be a small, bitter victory. This is neutralised, however, by the imagined 'wink'.

Extend Sample answer: The effects of the first-person perspective are quite varied. There is an immediate sense of a personal viewpoint which floods the poem with thoughts and feelings, giving a clear sense of a mind at work. The reader shares the flow of these thoughts and feelings and may have some sympathy with them, depending on their experience of life. There is a sense that the speaker is describing what she sees and also what she imagines. The reader has to accept the truth of the speaker's judgements. There are clues as to how the speaker herself comes across to others. 'Some acquaintance grabs your arm' suggests that her non-verbal communication is clearly signalling anger and jealousy despite her belief that her face is 'calm, expressionless'. This might make the reader feel that the speaker's judgements cannot be fully trusted.

Pages 25–27

Revise 1 Sample answers: **a)** '**You** must forgive **me**'; 'I have spoiled this body **we** once shared'; '**I**'d like to say **we** could be friends'; 'I won't keep **you** then'; 'I shan't cloud **your** morning'; 'I leave **you** in an ecstasy of concentration' **b)** 'Do **you** remember how …. **we**'d jump …'; 'That dream **we** had'; '**We** made a start'

Revise 2 Answers might include: **a)** physical activity/imaginative play, summer, natural world, intense/positive emotions **b)** injury, pain, fear, negativity

Revise 3 Answers might include: **a) (i)** 'Do you remember how …' **(ii)** 'You must forgive me.' **(iii)** 'Don't look so surprised …' **(iv)** 'the truth is we have nothing in common' **b) (i)** 'I won't keep you then.' **(ii)** 'I'd like to say we could be friends …'

Extend Sample answer: The final three lines describe a close-up image of the nine-year-old-self 'in an ecstasy of concentration', absorbed in 'peeling' a scab and then tasting it. The image is realistic and might remind many readers of similar childhood experiences, when the instinct to pick a scab and derive pleasure from doing so is very strong, overcoming any advice about healing or infection. The image is one of relative stillness compared to the playful activities associated with the younger self and captures something new about childhood and the natural instincts we learn to control as we get older.

Pages 28–29

Revise 1 Answers might include: nostalgic, haunted by the past, desiring love, yearning for her youth, emotional, sad, living in the past

Revise 2 Answers might include: **a)** The lonely tree (whose awareness of the loss of its birds is felt through it being 'more silent than before') is a metaphor for the speaker's loneliness and sense of absence. The birds are like the vague memories of the 'unremembered lads' which come to her like 'ghosts'. **b)** Winter is when the tree

is bare and the absence of birds is noticed through a lack of birdsong. It also relates to the 'winter' of the speaker's life, when she is old and physical love is only a memory. Summer is a metaphor for the temporary nature of youth and happiness which 'sang in me a / little while'. **c)** The last lines of the sestet move from past tense ('sang in me') to present tense ('in me sings no more'). This makes the final line full of pathos after the high emotion of 'sang'. The speaker remembers the feel of summer but not the detail of the loves that 'have come and gone' and knows that her loneliness is now a fixed state. The final two words, 'no more', close the sonnet with a deep sense of sadness.

Revise 3 a) The stress pattern in the volta is: 'THUS in the WINTer STANDS the LONEly TREE'. **b)** The stress on the first word 'thus' changes the rhythm of the first half of the line. It signals a shift in thinking as the speaker moves from her thoughts and emergent feelings to find an image for her emotions.

Extend Answers might include: The perspective, an older woman reflecting on her past and the many lovers she had, contrasts with the usual convention of a male perspective in a traditional love sonnet. In addition, her views and experiences are quite progressive for the time at which she wrote, the early 20th century.

Pages 30–31

Revise 1 Repeated references to 'my father' and 'my mother', 'my fingers' and 'my palms', 'by my (our) hands'. Repetition of longer phrases: 'My father's in/by'; 'my mother's in/by'. **b)** Answers might include: **parents:** mother, father; **human body:** hands, palms, fingers, skin, body, bodies; **marriage ceremony:** chapel, steeple, priests, psalms, marriage register, wedding; **apartness:** separate lands, separate hemispheres, 'nothing left of their togetherness', repelled, 'may sleep with other lovers'; **connection:** link, touch; **to make a new beginning:** take, take up

Revise 2 Answers might include: **a)** 'My father's in my fingers, but my mother's in my palms.' **b)** 'With nothing left of their togetherness …' **c)** 'My body is their marriage register.' **d)** 'So take me with you, take up the skin's demands …'

Revise 3 Sample answer: Repetition helps to convey the key theme of biological inheritance by drawing the reader's attention again and again to images of inherited 'fingers' and 'palms'. The effect is hypnotic and strange. The use of 'to separate lands, / To separate hemispheres' builds the theme of apartness by emphasising the parents' physical distance from each other. The parents could not be farther apart but in the speaker 'they touch, where fingers link to palms'. Some of the repetition is not the exact word repeated but a related one such as 'marriage' and 'wedding' which allows the theme to develop.

Extend Sample answer: The first-person perspective clarifies the key theme because the subject matter suits the expression of personal thoughts and feelings. It is an intimate poem which expresses powerful emotions about personal identity and the idea that children can be a lasting reminder of their parents' marriage. Even when the relationship is over, the evidence of the union resides in the genetic inheritance of their offspring. In the final verse, the shift from the first-person singular (I/my) to the first-person plural (We/our) signifies a union that the speaker is proposing with another which further extends the theme of heredity.

Pages 32–33

Revise 1 a) 'his plumage black'; 'his yellow bill'; 'kindled (against the sunset)'; 'rapt on his pinnacle of song'; 'figured above our garden plots' **b)** 'over the garden of the town'; 'his customary stack'; 'these suburbs'; 'above our garden plots'

Revise 2 Answers might include: **a)** '**chosen** evenings' implies the blackbird has the ability to make a decision; 'blackbird **bountiful**' implies that his visit and singing is a generous gift; '**customary** stack' implies his liking for a particular chimney stack. All these examples suggest that the blackbird has human attributes of decision-making, generosity and preference. **b)** '**divine** arithmetic' implies there is something spiritual or god-like about the blackbird as well as an ability to calculate numbers; '**Kindled** against the sunset' describes the effect of the setting sun, making the blackbird look as if he is on fire; '**Rapt** on his pinnacle of song' describes the blackbird as being absorbed and enchanted by his own singing; '**celestial** chimney-pots' suggests that there is a heavenly quality about something ordinary, made so by the blackbird. All these examples suggest that the blackbird has heavenly attributes and an ability to please, delight, arouse and inspire.

Revise 3 Sample answer: The blackbird symbolises beauty, intelligence and spirituality. First, his visits are elevated in the speaker's mind to special occasions, where the blackbird has a mysterious power to change the ordinary suburbs into an extraordinary place of beauty and wonder. The blackbird 'couches' before he 'lifts his yellow bill' which suggests he is getting into position. This process is noted by the speaker as a type of pre-performance preparation reinforcing a sense of the blackbird's intelligence. The blackbird's presence has a transformative effect on the suburban gardens, making them heavenly in the speaker's eyes, as if graced by the blackbird's presence.

Extend Sample answer: The speaker compares the suburban gardens to 'Dymock woods', a rural area west of Gloucester. The reader infers from the simile that the blackbird's presence has changed the mood of the suburban gardens, making them feel like a rural, isolated spot. The description of the woods as a place 'where music has her solitudes' personifies music as female and the word 'solitudes' suggests, in this context, away from the distractions of everyday life, rather than loneliness.

Pages 34–36

Revise 1 a) (i) There are two rhymes in the poem. The rhyme scheme is: a, a, a, b, b, b. **(ii)** There are eight syllables to a line. The dominant stress pattern is an unstressed syllable followed by a stressed one (di-dum): 'He CLASPS the CRAG with CROOKed HANDS.' **(iii)** There are four feet to a line and the metre is dominantly iambic tetrameter. **(iv)** the rhyming words are stressed **(v)** the second and third lines start with a stressed syllable. **b) (i)** alliteration – all begin with /c/, two begin with /cl/ and two with /cr/. The sounds are harsh and reflect the rugged strength of the eagle and its landscape. **(ii)** assonance, /a/ – establishes a link between the meaning of the words – both are distorted features. **(iii)** assonance, /o/ – establishes a link between the meaning of the words – both in context suggest ideas of uninhabited or inhospitable space. **(iv)** alliteration, /l/ – reinforces the remote and barren nature of the eagle's environment **(v)** alliteration, /r/, and assonance, /i/. Also, the first syllable of both words is very similar. The words have very different meanings, but both reinforce a sense of the eagle as a king of his domain. 'Ring'd' means both encircled by and wearing a ring, perhaps like a crown. 'Wrinkled' suggests an aerial view of the sea as the eagle looks down on his territory, the waves looking like lines or folds. **(vi)** alliteration, /w/ – links the act of watching with the place he is watching from, the wall, and therefore helps to build the image.

Revise 2 a) 'clasps', 'hands', 'stands', 'watches' **b)** 'close to the sun', 'ring'd with the azure world', 'wrinkled sea beneath him crawls', 'watches from his mountain walls', 'like a thunderbolt he falls' **c)** 'ring'd', 'stands', 'watches', 'like a thunderbolt'

Revise 3 Sample answer: The style of the poem is mostly **simple** and some meanings are **literal**, such as 'mountain wall'. Some descriptions are **precise** and **visual**, such as the verb 'clasps' and the adjective 'azure' to refer to the bright blue of a cloudless sky. Phrases such as 'lonely lands' and 'wrinkled sea' are more **complex** because a land cannot be 'lonely' nor a sea 'wrinkled'. Loneliness is a feeling and wrinkled usually describes skin or fabric so the style here is **metaphorical**, with comparisons being implied. The sound patterns in some of the words, such as the alliteration in 'ring'd' and 'wrinkled' and the assonance in 'crag' and 'hands', provide an important **aural** element to the poem's style.

Extend Sample answer: In the first triplet, the eagle is described as completely still. His strength and dormant energy are suggested by the verb 'clasped'. A regal, proud quality is suggested by 'ring'd with the azure world', as if the sky is a halo or crown. The verb 'stands' reflects his dominance.

The second triplet allows the reader to share the eagle's perspective of the 'wrinkled sea beneath him crawls'. The word 'beneath' and the verb 'crawls' link back to his kingly dignity and reinforce the idea that the rest of the world is below him and subservient. The shift from 'watches' to 'falls' is sudden and rapid as there is no mention of any transition between the two states and this reflects his predatory power. The simile 'like a thunderbolt' reinforces the sudden and unexpected nature of the movement and his destructive intent.

Pages 37–39

Revise 1 Answers might include any of the adjectives provided, depending on your interpretation of the tone and situation.

Revise 2 Answers might include: **a)** All the examples are imperative verbs, where the man is controlling the woman's actions and telling her to do something. **b)** All the examples are explanatory, some are statements of the obvious and some display specific knowledge that the man has and assumes or knows that the woman does not have. **c)** Both examples imply meaning that in the context is better left unsaid such as the function of 'soft roll' and the woman's caution around the mechanic's dog. **d)** Both examples can be understood as corrections, regulating the actions of the woman, although both can also be understood as advice.

Revise 3 Sample answer: The male persona uses the derogatory term of address 'love', which communicates his patronising attitude. (Another reading is that the term of address 'love' is a linguistic marker of friendliness and the cultural norm for many communities.) The language he uses to describe tools, car parts and the topping-up process is deliberately precise to showcase his knowledge and undermine her, for example 'five-eighths screwdriver', 'spade connector', 'clutch reservoir' and 'float chamber'. (Another reading is that he is helping a woman who wants to fix her own car, has the 'toolkit' to do so and understands his use of jargon.) After she has finished, the language he uses is more everyday, such as 'nothing of a job'. This switch in style can be interpreted as normal, as he is no longer describing a process, or perceived as contemptuous in that he is downplaying the process that he described in such detail, and which is, for him, a familiar and routine job. His final words 'Tell your husband' imply a view that car maintenance/repair is a male pursuit and an assumption that the woman is married.

Extend Sample answer: The title sounds conversational and is rather unusual for a poem. When the poem is read, the reader understands that this is something the male persona would say. It is also ironic as the two words 'very simply' would seem to signal a straightforward process when the reverse is the case. There is a gap between what is said and what is meant.

Pages 40–42

Revise 1 Answers might include: resigned, accepting, realistic, witty, amusing, untroubled, funny, at ease, untroubled, satisfied, unworried

Revise 2 a) The quotations are all conversational, idioms and sayings. **b)** The quotations provide humour as they are unusual, metaphorical word combinations. **c)** Answers might include: **(i)** 'Yes, he is the same as he usually is.' **(ii)** 'I know this is all very boring.' **(iii)** 'There was drama enough in my turbulent past'

Revise 3 Sample answer: Different aspects of the speaker are revealed as the poem develops. In the first stanza it feels as if her relationship is static and her life unfulfilled but it is soon apparent that, for her, 'new' is unattractive and familiar is preferable. There is a note of humour in 'and snoring' which signals a dominant tone of the poem. In the second stanza, there is a reference to the past as 'turbulent' which suggests conflict and instability. 'Tears and passion' are expressions of intense emotion and the persona admits that she has 'used up a tankful'. This hints at experiences which have worn her down. The casual nature of the language here possibly contradicts the intensity of the subject matter or is an effort to make fun of past distress as a coping mechanism. This raises questions about the persona and her level of contentment. The final stanza reveals the reasons why the persona avoids social gatherings. The list detailing the process of what happens during and after a party makes it sound meaningless. The fact that she has 'found a safe mooring' sounds more honest, as if she has found peace of mind in a stable relationship.

Extend Sample answer: The effect of rhyme on the poem is to make it sound comic and light-hearted. The effect of the epigram is to raise a question in the reader's mind about its relationship to the title and the poem itself. The words 'Chinese curse' anchor the meaning of the epigram and signal the poem's wry tone.

Pages 43–45

Revise 1 a) The narrator notices the other customers and what they are doing, his material surroundings and how the waitresses move. **b)** The effect of the lists on the poem's mood is to make the narrator's environment seem rather dull as if he is distanced and disconnected from the life he sees around him.

Revise 2 Answers might include:
a) Suggests both the possibility of someone else joining him and the narrator's awareness that this is not going to happen. **b)** The list suggests these actions are mechanical and that he misses social contact with another person. **c)** Both lines begin 'I'd like to' which reveals that his ideal world is one where he could 'talk' and possibly joke about the lily and enjoy being in a restaurant in the company of someone else, sharing thoughts and opinions about the sweet menu.

Revise 3 Answers might include: The only time any words are spoken is when the narrator places his order and is offered and declines the sweet menu. His only communication is restricted to the business in hand, expressed in the set formula of placing an order. The fact that he would like to spend time choosing and speak about his preferences, but is unable, reveals his loneliness and creates sympathy.

Extend Answers might include: The first-person narrator is in a social environment where he feels very aware of being alone. His thoughts and feelings are recorded

in a very precise way which feels rather strange. As the poem develops, the reader is made aware that he is doing this as he has no-one to distract him. He is focusing closely on his environment and what catches his attention. The comments about a family teaching a baby how to clap, a source of amusement for them, reinforces the narrator's solitariness. The style of the waitresses and their balletic movements ('spin', 'pirouettes', 'pliés') reveal the narrator's artistic eye and his appreciation of their grace. The final line, 'it hasn't come to much', is ambiguous as it has a literal meaning relating to the cost of the meal, but also feels as if it applies more widely to the narrator's perception of his life.

Pages 46–48

Revise 1 a) All the adjectives are useful for describing the persona of the hawk apart from 'happy' and 'loving'. **b)** Answers might include: **(i)** 'I am no longer free', 'I am blind to other birds' **(ii)** 'That when I go I go / At your commands' **(iii)** 'You but half-civilise, / Taming me in this way' **(iv)** 'You seeled me with your love … The habit of your words / Has hooded me' **(v)** 'Through having only eyes / For you I fear to lose' **(vi)** 'I am blind to other birds'; 'But only want the feel …' **(vii)** 'and choose / Tamer as prey'

Revise 2 a) 'but gentled at your hands' **b)** 'I am no longer free' **c)** 'cannot be quick enough to fly for you' **d)** 'I am blind to other birds' **e)** 'you seeled me with your love' **f)** 'but only want the feel …'

Revise 3 Answers might include: **Stanza 1:** The hawk refers to the past when they were wild and free and how they are now tamed. **Stanza 2:** The hawk refers to the present and reflects on how, even when they fly, they are not free because they have been tamed and blinded. **Stanza 3:** The hawk describes the movements they can make when in the air but how they feel different now that they are tamed. **Stanza 4:** The hawk refers to their state as somewhere between wild and tame and asserts their power to choose, even if it is a choice to be tamed.

Extend The rhyme scheme is a, b, a, c, c, b. The metre is iambic trimeter for the first five lines of each stanza, e.g. 'I THOUGHT I WAS so TOUGH'. The last short line of each stanza is iambic tetrameter, e.g. 'uPON your WRIST'. The strict rhyme scheme and the metre harmonise with the subject matter which is about control and constraint. The short taut statements, governed by the poem's metre, draw attention to the hawk's lack of freedom, e.g. 'I am no longer free'. The final b rhyme of the first stanza ('commands'), linking back to 'hands', emphasises the tamer's verbal and physical power over the hawk.

Pages 49–51

Revise 1 a) All the adjectives are useful for describing the setting. **b)** Sample answer: The setting is **bleak** and **desolate** with the speaker vulnerable to the elements. The line 'their bare boughs weighed with snow' shows that it is **wintry** and the snowfall has been heavy and extensive. **c) (i)** 'But a tyrant spell has bound me' **(ii)** 'The night is darkening round

me' **(iii)** 'Clouds beyond clouds above me, / Wastes beyond wastes below' **(iv)** 'And I cannot, cannot go.' / 'And yet I cannot go.' **(v)** 'But nothing drear can move me; / I will not, cannot go.'

Revise 2 a) The rhyme scheme is: a, b, a, b, c, b, c, b, a, b, a, b. The 'b' end rhyme of each quatrain reinforces the speaker's isolation and inability to move. **b)** The metre is irregular. The longer lines (the first and third in each quatrain) are seven or eight syllables long. The shorter lines (the second and fourth in each quatrain) are six or seven syllables long. **c)** Some lines are iambic trimeter (six syllables following an unstressed and stressed pattern, e.g. The WILD winds COLDly BLOW / I WILL not CANnot GO). Some lines with seven syllables have an iambic trimeter pattern with an extra unstressed syllable at the end (e.g. The NIGHT is DARKening ROUND me). Some lines that break the iambic pattern do so right at the beginning, where the first word signals a contrast in meaning (e.g. BUT a TYrant SPELL has BOUND me). **d)** The other sound patterns are: alliteration ('wild winds', 'bare boughs') and assonance ('coldly blow'). Their effect is to draw attention to the meaning of the words. All the examples of alliteration and assonance reinforce the harsh weather or its effects on the landscape.

Revise 3 Sample answer: There are three sentences in the poem, one in each quatrain. Each sentence is divided into two parts by a semi-colon, which marks an emphatic pause connecting the meaning of the two parts. The first part of the sentence describes the situation and makes reference to the natural world. The second part counters the first part by the use of 'but' or 'and yet'.

The poem has a clear narrative structure. Each quatrain has a part to play in the story. The first quatrain describes the setting and the situation of the trapped speaker. The second develops the story by providing more details of the setting and reinforces the vulnerability of the speaker's situation. The third quatrain suggests that the speaker's situation is complicated by a desire to stay rather than an inability to go. Another way of understanding the narrative is to see it as more circular, with each quatrain saying the same thing with only minor variation. The poem has many structural patterns: sound (alliteration and assonance), and repetition of words, phrases and punctuation. These repetitive, memorable patterns create a strong sense of an intense, continuous and unchanging situation. The speaker's problem is expressed but not solved. There is no moving on.

Extend Sample answer: The speaker's emotional state is suggested by the details of the external setting. The speaker is alone and exposed to the power of the elements in a setting which is cold, bleak and oppressive. The line 'the night is darkening 'round me' puts her at the centre and suggests feelings of entrapment. The repetition of 'wastes' reinforces the setting's inhospitable nature. Many of the nouns are in the plural form ('winds', 'trees', 'boughs', 'clouds' and 'wastes'), suggesting the massed force of nature pitted against an individual who is feeling isolated and vulnerable.

Pages 52–54

Revise 1 Answers might include: **a)** 'Traffic holding its breath' **b)** 'With nervous childish talk' **c)** 'Deployed our talk with art' **d)** 'Still waters running deep'

Revise 2 Answers might include: **a)** The personification of the traffic suggests the idea of waiting for something to happen, as if the traffic is their audience. **b)** The diaphragm is a metaphor for the strained atmosphere of excitement around and above them. **c)** The simile compares the falling evening light to a dark stage backdrop, perhaps also suggesting their careful role play. **d)** The simile compares the couple to a hawk and prey who have not yet come together but it is unclear who is predator and who is prey. **e)** Mushroom is a metaphor for previous love that had sprung up too quickly and exploded, resulting in feelings of revulsion and hostility. **f)** The simile emphasises the wariness between them, one a small to medium-sized songbird and the other a much larger bird of prey, a hawk, who might take the other by surprise. **g)** The behaviour of the young couple is outwardly calm to the objective eye, like 'still waters', but underlying this there is strength of feeling and possibly passion 'running deep'.

Revise 3 Sample answer: 'Twice Shy' refers to the proverb/saying 'Once bitten, twice shy', which means that a difficult experience, such as being hurt in a relationship, makes a person very cautious. The title provides some guidance for the reader as it suggests that there is a backstory to this relationship but no detail is given as to whether one or both have been hurt in the past or by whom.

Extend Sample answer: The opening stanza describes the female character through appraising male eyes. The speaker precisely notes the details of her appearance. The opening line, 'Her scarf à la Bardot' lends her an exotic, sexual glamour. 'Suede flats' suggests a compromise between dressiness and practicality. The scene is set in broad terms of time and place: 'one evening', 'the quiet river' and 'the embankment walk'. The reason behind the walk, 'for air and friendly talk', appears to downplay its significance. The noun 'walk' is repeated, which draws the reader's attention, and

the verbs are all those of related actions: 'came', 'crossed' and 'took'. The language of the final stanza is very different as there are more words relating to emotions rather than actions. 'Chary', 'excited', 'thrilled' and 'nervous' are all intense feelings. The first stanza is full of literal descriptions whereas the final one is metaphorical. The couple are likened to very different types of birds, a 'thrush linked on a hawk', with the verb 'linked on' suggesting that they are walking closely together. The metaphor of the river and 'still waters running deep' suggests their underlying feelings for each other. The final two words, 'embankment walk', take the reader back to the end of the first stanza. There is a circularity here but also a sense that the situation between them has changed.

Pages 55–56

Revise 1 a) The rhyme scheme is a, b, a, b, c, b, c, b, d, b, d, b. The 'b' rhyme occurs on every alternate line. **b)** The continuity of the 'b' rhymes, the variation of the 'a', 'c' and 'd' rhymes and the regular, emphatic rhythm echoes the steady, pounding drum-like beat of wheels on rails.

Revise 2 Answers might include: **First lines:** establish what the speaker is thinking and perceiving and add some contextual information (e.g. in the first quatrain, the reader learns that the train track is 'miles away' and therefore in the speaker's imagination, not close by). **Second lines:** develop the thought stated in the first line. They all begin with a linking word ('and' or 'though'). They add more description (e.g. 'the night is still' in the second quatrain contrasts with 'the day is loud' in the first quatrain). **Third lines:** signal a different line of thinking by the linking words 'yet' and 'but'. They all share a similar meaning – in spite of the train's physical distance from the speaker, she clearly imagines its presence, hears it, sees it and, in the case of the third quatrain, wants to go on it. **Fourth lines:** emphasise the reality, power and lure of the train in the speaker's imagination.

Revise 3 Sample answer: The final quatrain reveals that the speaker is fascinated by the possibilities of train travel and the lure of somewhere new, and this desire overrides the 'warm' affection she feels for friends at home. The train appears to symbolise a need to explore the unfamiliar rather than a desire to escape.

Extend Sample answer: The repetitive statement 'there isn't a train' makes this key idea more memorable and emphatic. It is also hyperbolic as the speaker is developing the idea that any train or any train journey is a good one in her view. It suggests the speaker's idealistic enthusiasm and obsession about the positive prospect of train travel regardless of its possible negative realities.

Pages 57–58

Revise 1 Answers might include: the non-verbal interjection 'Shhh'; the phrase 'with respect'; the colloquial expression 'a good old chat'; the telegraphic statement 'obviously nothing to do with mobiles' (instead of 'they obviously have nothing …'); the series of rhetorical questions.

Revise 2 Sample answer: The speaker's tone is both **humorous** and **ironic**. The extended list of rhetorical questions provides some colourful imagery to express the speaker's annoyance at the woman's ignorance or lack of sensitivity. The speaker's **disapproval** is also clear from the exaggerated language such as 'horde' and 'stampede', which ridicules the woman's lack of awareness.

Revise 3 Sample answer: The poem is divided into four sections of uneven lengths because it reflects the structures of unspoken thought rather than writing. The first and final sections frame the poem, the opening stanza setting the scene and the final one emphasising the difficulty some people have in saying what they mean. The middle section of the poem shows the workings of the speaker's mind as she silently asks a series of questions. The speaker's imagination runs free, contrasting with the usual polite restraint that characterises conversations between strangers on a train.

Extend Answers should include: The words in italics under the title act as a mock dedication to the woman featured in the poem. It also orients the reader who is given some contextual background before the poem begins. The detail contained in the italicised words, such as the route of the train, also suggests that this episode is drawn from real-life experience.

Answers – Exam Preparation

Pages 59–62

Revise 1

The poet uses the perspective of a son looking back on his childhood and remembering the work his father did in the home, on winter Sundays as well as during the week. The feelings presented about the hardworking father are all tinged with negativity: sadness, regret and guilt.

Answers might include:
The key words of the question are all used – 'poet', 'present' and 'feelings about the father'.
The second sentence lists the feelings and what they have in common – provides an overview.

Revise 2

❶The opening lines establish a subdued tone and mood, generated by the feelings expressed about the father. ❷'Sundays too …' implies that the speaker's father worked to support and care for his family on Sundays as on every other day. The striking ❸image of soreness and the effects of hard manual ❹'labour' in the father's ❺'cracked hands' is linked, through ❻assonance, with the image of ❼'banked fires blaze'. The power of this second image is enhanced by the strong /b/ ❽alliteration. The speaker is quietly and sadly acknowledging his father's efforts. The closing statement of the first stanza, ❾'No one ever thanked him', is an admission of guilt because the speaker includes ❿himself.

⓫The speaker's feelings about his father are bound up with his behaviour as a child and the home atmosphere. The ⓬past tense 'I'd wake' reinforces the idea of looking back, but also ⓭suggests habitual actions, what the speaker ⓮'would' regularly do. The ⓯descriptive language is quite simple, such as the speaker getting up 'slowly' once the house has warmed up. His leisurely behaviour ⓰contrasts with the father's purposeful activity. The descriptive language in 'fearing the chronic angers of the house' is more complex as it is ⓱unexplained and out of place with the fire's warmth. A negative ⓲mood persists, unattached to an individual.

⓳The final stanza foregrounds the negative feelings attached to the speaker's relationship with the father. The ⓴adverb 'indifferently' describes the speaker's manner which he now regrets. The physical force ㉑implied in 'driven out the cold' and the ㉒afterthought of the polishing of 'my good shoes as well' echoes the meaning of 'too' at the start of the poem, ㉓emphasising the amount of work the father did for the family and the speaker in particular. The poem concludes with an emotional ㉔repeated question, 'What did I know, what did I know …?' The speaker's tone here is one of ㉕regret and sadness.

Answers might include:
1. Topic sentence on the overall mood of the poem and how it is generated.
2. embedded quotation
3. method
4. embedded quotation
5. embedded quotation
6. method
7. embedded quotation
8. method
9. embedded quotation
10. The first paragraph makes an important point that the narrator feels guilt and sadness that his father's hard work was unacknowledged at the time.
11. Topic sentence on feelings and their connection with childhood and home life.
12. method
13. suggested meaning
14. use of modal 'would' reinforces the idea of looking back
15. method
16. method and meaning
17. linked to meaning
18. method
19. Topic sentence signals a focus on the final stanza and the feelings expressed.
20. method
21. implied meaning
22. linked to meaning
23. linked to meaning
24. method
25. linked to meaning – tone

Revise 3

The feelings presented have a ❶powerful emotional effect on the speaker and this transfers to the reader. The ending implies the speaker now understands that these 'offices' were acts of love. ❷It makes the reader consider how love is understood and communicated and how time and experience help us to see life more clearly.

Answers might include:
1. This key idea does not repeat any phrasing from earlier.
2. Sums up the effect of the poem on the reader and shows empathy and understanding.

Revise 1

Sample answer in which the first paragraph is now more tightly organised and the quotations are embedded: The poet uses the form of the Petrarchan sonnet to present London's beauty and grandeur. He uses descriptive language, for example the adjective 'fair'. The line 'never did sun more beautifully steep' evokes a picture of the city in the early morning sun, almost being soaked by the sunlight. The adjectives 'bright' and 'glittering' also describe the quality of the light. The descriptive language is positive, reinforcing the speaker's pleasure in the city's appearance.

Revise 2

Answers might include: The 7+ response is more detailed; points are more confidently developed; the paragraphs have stronger topic sentences; there is a precise use of terminology such as 'octave' and 'sestet'; the meanings of figurative language, such as simile and personification, are explored more fully; there is a wider range of methods selected for comment; all the quotations are carefully embedded.

Revise 1

a) Answers might include: **Strengths:** clearly organised; clearly expressed. **Weaknesses:** some sentences are rather short and abrupt; some points lack development. **b)** Sample answer – an improvement to paragraph 1: The poems show marked contrast in the way the observers express their feelings. Wordsworth's speaker is full of praise for London ❶whereas Lowell's speaker is full of dread. In 'Composed on Westminster Bridge, September 3, 1802', the speaker focuses solely on London's beauty in the early morning sunshine. In 'A London Thoroughfare. 2am', Lowell's speaker describes London as an 'alien city' in the dark hours of the early morning. ❷London is presented in an appealing way in Wordsworth's poem, using a lexical set of beauty: 'fair', 'beauty' and 'beautifully'. In Lowell's poem, ❸however, London is presented as an eerie city. ❹The adjectives 'cold' and 'barred', for example, make London appear hostile, like a prison.

1. Points are linked more clearly
2. Point is developed with examples
3. A different linking word is used to signal a contrast
4. Sentences are longer and more fully developed

Revise 2

Answers might include: The 7+ response is more detailed; paragraphs are longer and points are better developed; examples are provided to support the main points; there is greater use of terminology to describe methods and their effects; the argument is more confident; the style is more sophisticated and the expression is more fluent.

Revise 1

Answers might include: **a)** At the beginning, the speaker describes the bird as 'My blackbird' as if the bird belongs to him or as if he feels a personal connection between himself and the blackbird. The adjective 'bountiful' suggests the generosity of the blackbird, as if he is a gift to the speaker. **b)** The blackbird is presented in a suburban setting conveyed by the imagery of 'garden plots' and 'chimney-pots'. **c)** The blackbird's appearance is described literally and simply with his 'plumage black' and 'yellow bill'. **d)** At the end, the poet creates a clear image of the blackbird 'figured above our garden plots' as if in a painting.

Revise 2

Answers might include: **a)** At the beginning, the poet presents the group of blackbirds 'perched in flocks' in the early autumn. **b)** The blackbirds are presented in a garden in a hickory tree, which feels rural. **c)** The blackbirds' appearance is compared to 'a sable shower', like black rain. **d)** The blackbirds' behaviour is compared to a 'flittering, noisy, chattering crowd'. **e)** The two metaphors compare the blackbirds to the natural world and the human world. The words 'sable shower', 'flittering', 'noisy' 'chattering' and 'crowd' convey the idea of light movement and loud, excitable behaviour.

Revise 3

Similarities: The appearance of the blackbirds – they are described literally, e.g. their colour, and metaphorically, e.g. through personification. Both poems use a first-person speaker who watches out for the blackbirds and has an emotional response to their presence. Differences: The appearance of the blackbirds – different colour words are used. The first is more literal, using basic colour words, whereas the second is more poetic, using 'sable', a more precise colour, and combining it with 'shower' to make the description metaphorical. The behaviour of the blackbirds – single blackbird with irregular visits, but always following the same pattern (a song), versus a group that make daily visits. The sounds of the blackbirds – song (a performance) versus 'loud talk' and 'chattering' (to each other). The metaphors used to describe the sounds in the second poem emphasise the blackbirds' social behaviour, whereas those used in the first emphasise the beauty of the blackbird's song. The effect of the blackbirds – uplifted versus saddened by their absence.

Revise 4

Similarities: Both poems use personification as a descriptive device. In the first poem, the words 'chosen' and 'bountiful' give the blackbird qualities of decision making and generosity. Similarly, the second poem uses 'chattering' and 'talked' to suggest the blackbirds' human-like communication. The use of personification in both poems helps to give the blackbirds a character.

The poems also share another similarity in that they both make use of the first-person speaker whose observation of the blackbirds leads to an emotional response. In the first poem, the phrase 'my blackbird' conveys personal affection. In the second poem, the speaker watches the blackbirds 'hour by hour' and associates their absence with a lack of knowledge, 'little I know what awaiteth me'.

Differences: The use of colour to describe the appearance of the blackbirds is different. In the first poem, the colours 'black' and 'yellow' are simple and straightforward, whereas in the second poem the colour is more unusual. 'Sable' suggests both dark brown and black and also the soft texture of fur from the animal of the same name.

Another contrast is how frequently the blackbirds visit. In the first poem, the blackbird comes on 'chosen evenings'. His appearance is less predictable than the blackbirds of the second poem who come 'day after day'. This difference is important for the meaning of the poems. The less frequent appearance of the blackbird in the first poem makes his visits 'bountiful', like a gift. The regularity of the blackbirds' presence in the second poem creates an expectation and their absence generates a 'sorrowful thought'.

Revise 5

Both poems share similar subject matter as they are about blackbirds. The first poem focuses on a solitary blackbird, referred to as 'he,' but the second focuses on a group, described as both a 'flock' and a 'crowd'. The blackbird of the first poem is individualised whereas the 'noisy' 'chattering' blackbirds of the second poem are not, as they all behave in the same way.

Revise 6

Similarities: similarly, likewise, also, in the same way, both, despite these differences, along the same lines

Differences: on the other hand, in contrast, despite these similarities, however, whereas, conversely, even though

Revise 7

❶The first poem presents a positive image of the solitary male blackbird who appears on 'chosen evenings'. In the suburban setting, with its 'chimneys thick', his presence feels 'bountiful', like a personal gift to the speaker. ❷In the second poem, a 'crowd' of blackbirds are presented in the 'hickory tree' of the speaker's garden, which feels more isolated and rural. The presentation of these blackbirds ❸is also positive, ❹but their absence at the end is associated with sadness. ❺Both speakers are affected by the birds and this gives the poems their emotional power.

1. First poem introduced with a summary of its key features
2. Second poem introduced with a summary of its key features
3. A similarity introduced
4. A difference introduced
5. Similarity introduced with some development

Sample answers:

Method 1: The first poem has an uplifting mood as the speaker describes the positive effect that the blackbird has on his feelings and perceptions. The simile 'these suburbs are like Dymock woods' reveals how the blackbird's song has transported the speaker from a suburban garden to a rural idyll. The speaker is fascinated by the behaviour of the blackbird and his wonder is conveyed in the phrase 'by some divine arithmetic'. The poem has a dominant tone of admiration which builds as the poem develops.

The mood of the second poem is more subdued and feels very different to the first poem. The speaker seems more isolated and the tone of the voice changes from curiosity to sadness when the blackbirds leave. The speaker refers to her 'sorrowful thought' and watches 'sadly' as the leaves fall, winter begins and the blackbirds leave. The ending implies that the blackbirds coming and going are a reminder to the speaker of time passing and a lack of knowledge about her future. This low-key ending contrasts with the optimism of the first poem.

Method 2: The mood of the two poems is different. The first is uplifting, with its speaker describing the blackbird's positive effect, whereas the second poem is much more subdued. In 'Blackbird', the simile 'these suburbs are like Dymock woods' reveals how the blackbird's song has transported the speaker from a suburban garden to a rural idyll. In contrast, the speaker in 'Blackbirds' watches 'sadly' as the leaves fall, winter begins and the blackbirds leave. The first speaker is fascinated by the blackbird's behaviour, conveying wonder in the phrase 'by some divine arithmetic'. On the other hand, for the second speaker, the blackbirds' coming and going is a reminder of time passing and a lack of knowledge about her own future. The first poem has a dominant tone of admiration building strongly as the poem develops, whereas the second poem begins positively with the speaker's curiosity but becomes gradually more sad.

Sample answers:

Method 1: The first poem describes a blackbird's visits to the suburbs and has some story-like features. The blackbird, for example, is the main character of the story as his actions are the focus for the first-person speaker. It is written in the present tense which reflects the current habit of the blackbird as if the reader is sharing the moment with the speaker. The climax of the story is the blackbird's song and its powerful effect on the speaker. The second poem also tells a story, of blackbirds visiting the speaker's garden every day until early winter, the present moment. The blackbirds are the collective main character of the story, in a similar way to the individual blackbird of the first poem. Their actions are also the focus of the first-person speaker's observations. The climax is the day when the speaker realises that the blackbirds have 'fled'.

The second poem has a clearer narrative than the first because it is a ballad set in the past and each quatrain pushes on the story. The first line of each quatrain shows the passage of time, for example 'day after day' and 'still they came'. The quatrains break up the story and make it easy to follow. The first poem is one long stanza formed of two sentences. The first sentence, the first four lines, introduces the blackbird and the timing of his arrival. The second sentence, comprising twelve lines, tells the reader more about where the blackbird settles, how he sings and his effect on the speaker. This extended sentence becomes more intense until it reaches its positive climax in 'those are celestial chimney-pots'. In contrast, the climax in the second poem expresses a wistful feeling about life's mystery, 'But, little I know what awaiteth me …!'

Method 2: Both poems are first-person narratives which concern the habits of blackbirds. The first tells the story in the present tense and focuses on the continuing habit of a blackbird's visit. The second is set in the recent past and describes the repeated visits of blackbirds over a passage of time up until the present moment. The blackbird or blackbirds are the main characters and their actions are the key focus for both speakers. Both poems have a climax, with the first poem's building up to the powerful effect of the blackbird's song and the second poem's expression of sadness at the blackbirds' failure to return.

The poems are different in form and this affects narrative structure. The first is one long stanza made up of two sentences, whereas the second is a ballad made up of quatrains that push on the story. The first line of each quatrain shows the passage of time, for example 'day after day' and 'still he came'. The narrative is broken up into small chunks for the reader. In contrast, the first sentence of the first poem is four lines long and introduces the blackbird and the timing of his arrival. The second sentence is twelve lines long and tells the reader more about where the blackbird settles, how he sings and his effect on the speaker. This second extended sentence becomes more intense until it reaches its climax in 'those are celestial chimney-pots'. In contrast, the second poem's climax is a wistful expression of life's mystery, 'But little I know what awaiteth me …!'

Revise 10

Sample answer: The first poem is one stanza although the rhyming couplets of a, a, b, b aid understanding by segmenting information. The rhymes are interesting because they are not obvious, for example 'evenings' and 'sings' and 'thick' and 'arithmetic'. The metre is mostly iambic tetrameter but the pattern varies, making the poem more conversational. The lines that break the pattern begin with striking words like 'kindled' and 'rapt'. The second poem is organised into quatrains, with alternate lines rhyming, which, like the rhyming couplets of the first poem, help to segment information. The poem's rhyme scheme, a, b, a, b, such as 'came' and 'flame', is typical of a ballad. The metre is loose as line length varies, unlike the tighter line lengths of the first poem. This also enhances the spoken quality of the poem.

Revise 11

Sample 1 Conclusion: In conclusion, both poems present the blackbirds as ❶behaving in a mysterious way. ❷In the first poem, this mystery is combined with a religious type of wonder, whereas in the second the mystery is combined with personal sadness when the blackbirds leave. The line 'But, little I know what awaiteth me', towards the end of the second poem, expresses a universal fear about life's mysteries. ❸The first poem implies that the mystery is connected with the 'divine' and would appeal to readers who share that belief. ❹The second poem is easy to understand because of its language, structure and form; its message about what is known and not known about life would resonate with many readers, including myself.

Sample 2 Conclusion: In conclusion, there are many similarities and differences between the two poems. The appearance, sound and behaviour of the blackbirds are described in detail in both poems. The poems both include first-person speakers who are affected by the visits of the blackbirds, as has already been indicated in this essay. ❺I prefer the first poem as I like the special one-to-one relationship between the speaker and the solitary blackbird. The second poem feels a bit old-fashioned with words like 'ere' and 'awaiteth' and appeals to me less. I also like the upbeat tone of the first poem whereas the second poem leaves me feeling a bit sad.

Which is the better response? Sample 1 is the better response as it avoids repeating the main points of the essay, unlike sample 2. Sample 1 also gives a view on the similarities and differences by evaluating the message of the two poems whereas Sample 2 does not. Both responses provide a personal response to the poems but do so differently. Sample 1 is a more sophisticated personal overview whereas sample 2 provides some useful examples of features they liked and disliked.

1. Brief overview.
2. This is developed further, with a contrast made about the mood underlying the mystery.
3. The first poem is understood to appeal to a specific audience, sharing the beliefs expressed in the poem.
4. The accessibility of the second poem and its message is commented upon and a personal response expressed.
5. Some personal response to content, style and tone is evident here.

Notes